ISBN: 81-7320-011-4

First Published 1993

Published by
AGAM KALA PRAKASHAN
34 Central Market, Ashok Vihar
Delhi-110052 Phone: 7113395

Laser Typeset by
QUICK PRINTS
2/8, Lajpat Nagar-4, Delhi-110024

Printed in India at New Prints, Delhi-110034

Dedicated
to
Padmashree Prof. V. Venkatachalam
and
Shrimati V. Gomathy

TABLE OF CONTENTS

PREFACE

Buddhism first spread in Tibet during the time of the Tibetan royal empire (mid-seventh century to mid-ninth century A.D.) which produced the majority of translations of Indian Buddhist treatises and the codification of this literature in Tibetan Buddhist canon, consisting of the *bka'-'gyur* and *bstan-'gyur* text-collections. During this period the political power in Tibet rested in the hands of the *sa-skya-pa* sect and a related dynasty in *gtsaṅ province*.

The third phase (sixteenth to eighteenth century A.D.) corresponds to the *dge-lugs-pa* sect. Their spiritual leader was the head of the Tibetan state from the mid-seventeenth century onwards. Their political power was initially strengthened by their close ties with Mongol Kings, particularly the Manchu dynasty.

During these three phases there are clear close indications that the Tibetan rulers acted as patrons to the Sanskrit studies in Tibet. The study of Indic lingustic disciplines mainly carried out in connection with the creation of the Indo-Tibetan translaion-literature. The Tibetan King's patronage of the Sanskrit studies inthe first phase helped considerably in formation of the Central Committee of Translators which was responsible for revision and standardization of the translations and for the compilaiton of the normatic Sanskrit-Tibetan lexicon the Mahāvyutpatti and its commentary entitled *sgra-sbyor-bam-po-gñis-pa*. In the latter book various aspects of Sanskrit grammar were included. In the next two phases the politically dominant sects—the *sa-skya-pa* and *dge-lugs-pa* were strong factors in the development of Sanskrit grammatical studies in Tibet. They were the only sects engaged in learning the Sanskrit Grammar. The contribution of the *dge-lugs-pa* sect to the development of Sanskrit linguistic studies lies mainly in the activities of the Fifth Dalai Lama Ṅag-dbaṅ-blo-bzaṅ-rgya-mtsho (1617-1682) and his regent Sde-srid-saṅs-rgyas-rgya-mtsho (1653-1705) both of them were responsible for an important revival of interest in various Indian art and sciences.

The majority of the materials on Sanskrit grammar found in the Tibetan Buddhist canon were translated during the second phase. To this phase belong the following works: CH II/1, CH III/1-11, 14-16, CH IV/1-13 and CH VII/1-6. These titles evidently formed part of the first version of the *bstan-'gyur* written in mid-fourteen century A.D. The rest of the work were translated in the last and third phase (i.e. CH II/2-4; CH III/17-19, CH V/1-3 and CH VI/1-2). Thus a total numer of forty-seven works were translated into Tibetan.

These works may, further, be divided into five grammatical schools i.e. Pāṇini, Cāndra, Kalāpa or Kātantra, Sārasvata and Mañjuśrī. However six works (CH VII/1-6) are not affiliated to any grammartical system. While the first four grammatical systems are quite popular in India, the last and the fifth one is obscure in Indian grammatical tradition. However, according to colphon of the text, a commentary on the system was compsed by Rājadeva, a king of Kaliṅga, modern Orissa.

There are seven chapters in this treatise on the system of Sanskrit Grammar in Tibet. The first chapter incorporated a study on the ninth-century work *sgra-sbyor-bam-po-gñis-pa*. In the first chapter it is discussed that the borrowing of elements from the Indian traditions of linguistic description are merely subservient to the development and perfection of the Tibetan translating-techniques.

The second chapter contents a brief history of Sanskrit grammar in general which is known both from the Indian and the Tibetan sources. It has been clearly projected that while Indians believe that *Śiva* was the tutelary deity of Pāṇini, the Tibetan traditions suggest that Lokeśvara was the tutelary deity. Besides, this chapter bears a study on four works on Pāṇinian system, those were translated into Tibetan by both Indian and Tibetan scholars.

Nineteen grammatical works on Cāndra system of Sanskrit grammar have been incorporated in the third chapter of the treatise. The Tibetan scholar Bu-ston states that Candragomin, the author of the Cāndra sūtra-text was born in Eastern India, in Bengal, without mentioning a more specific place name, but

Tāranātha an early 16th century Tibetan Historian and Koṅ-sprul Blo-gros-mthà-yas, a great scholar of nineteenth century A.D., have suggested Varendra as the birth-place of Candragomin. Koṅ-sprul Blo-gros-mtha'-yas further describes the episode where Candragomin despairs of the qualities of his own grammar after comparing it with a grammar entitled *Samantabhadra* composed by Candrakīrti. He threw his work in the well. On the intervention of his tutelary deity (Lokeśvara) according to (Bu-); Tārā according to (Tā-and Kon-) Candragomin decided to recover his grammar from the well which he had thrown. As the tutelary deity had prophesied, Cāndra grammar floruished, but the *Samantabhadra* grammar was waned. No Sanskrit grammatical treatise entitled *Samantabhadra* is known to have been preserved; but there is mention of *kin-tu-bzaṅ-po'i-byā-ka-ra-ṇa* (i.e. Skt. Samantabhadra Vyākaraṇa) in the Colophon of two grammatical treatises in the Tibetan canon (viz. *sum-cu-pa* and *rtags-kyi-'jug-pa*).

Next to Candragomin the most prominent Sanskrit grammatical systems in Tibet was Kalāpa or Kātantra system. The works affiliated to this system are being discussed in the fourth chapter. In the Tibetan canon we find thirteen grammatical works on Kalāpa system of Sanskrit grammar. Before presenting these thirteen works, a brief history of this grammatical system has been discussed in fourth chapter. Kārttikeya or Kumāra-ṣaṇmukha is the tutelary deity of Śarvavarman, the author of this grammatical sūtra-text. According to the Tibetan traditions god merely uttered *siddha varṇasamāmnāya* (Ka.I-1-1) after which all grammar in the synoptic form was clear to Śarvavarman. It is interesting to mark that this grammatical system has no pratyāhāras to denote groups of phonemes therefore there are no *Śiva-sūtras* at the beginnings. Kalāpa exclusively bases references to (groups of) phonemes on the traditional order of the Sanskrit alphabets. Exactly this traditional order of the alphabets is intended with the term *Varṇasamāmnāya*.

In the fifth chapter only three works have been discussed. These works belong to the Sārasvata system of Sanskrit Grammar. Anubhuti-svarūpācārya, a Maharastrian Brahmin is said to have been the author of the sūtra-text of this system. His text book is considered to have been revealed to him by the goddess Sarasvatī, hence the title Sarasvatī-vyākaraṇa or Sārasvatī-vyākaraṇa 'grammar made by Sarasvatī'.

A new system of Sanskrit grammar which is quite unknown in the Indian tradition of the history of Sanskrit grammar has been dealt with in the Sixth chapter. Only two works of this systems are known to us from the Tibetan canon i.e bstan-'gyur. Koṅ-sprul attributes the basic text of the grammatical system to Mañjuśrīkīrti. In the canonical editions the title of this text is Mañjuśrīśabda-lakṣaṇa and it is attributed to Sādhukīrti.

The seventh and the last chapter of this treatise bears a study on six grammatical works which are not affiliated to any system of Sanskrit grammar. This chapter includes two works on Sanskrit grammatical philosophy (i.e CH VII/3-4).

During the analysis of the original manuscripts, some variations in the cone version have been marked in this work. In the introduction chapter also the analysis of some grammatical elements like paraphase, separation of constituents of Sanskrit compound terms, semantic isolation of suffixes, morphological isolation of suffixes and isolation of verbal roots have mentioned. These things are not my contribution to this work, or these are taken from an unpublished thesis of pieter cornelis verhagen entitled "Sanskrit grammatical Literature in Tibet". The thesis has been presented to me by Prof. Dr. J. Bronkhorst, one of the promotor of the thesis. Thus, I am highly thankful to Prof. J. Bronkhorst (Switzerland) and pieter cornelis verhagen for their help and kindness.

My sincere thanks are due to the authorities of National Library, Calcutta. The Asiatic Society of Bengal, Calcutta; Oriental Institute, Baroda; Bhandarkar Oriental Institute, Pune; Library of Tibetan works and Archives, Dharmasala; Central Library, Visva-Bharti; Seminar Library of Indo-Tibetan Studies, Visva-Bharti; Library of B.L. Institute of Indology, Delhi; Orissa State Museum (Ms. Section), Bhubaneswar; Library of K.P. Jayswal Research Institute, Patna; Tibet House, New Delhi and Personal Library of Late Professor Sujeet Kumar Mukherjee, Santiniketan.

I am indebted to Prof. B.N. Banerjee and Dr. Dipak Bhattacharya (my Ph. D. Supervisor) of the Dept. of Sanskrit, for their valuable suggetions and advice. To work on this usbject I got the inspiration from my teacher Late Dr. Biswanath Bhattacharya when I was a student in the Dept. of Sanskrit (1982-84), Visva Bharati and since then I had been collecting materials for the present work.

Now, I am happy to record my deep thanks and sense of gratitude to Prof. N.C. Ghosh and Mrs. Manasi Ghosh, whose constant encoragement and inspiration were always in favour of me, while I was preparing the present monograph.

I am also thankful to Sj. Lama Chimpa and Sj. Suniti Pathak of the Deparment of Indo-Tibetan Studies, Visva-Bharti, from whom I learned Tibetan language and literature which enable me to study the Tibetan manuscripts and to analyse those in the present work. I do not hesitate to admit that Sj. Lama Chimpa had carefully revised the whole work and advised for minor changes.

Lastly, I am greatful to Dr. Agam Prasad, Proprietor, Agam Kala Prakashan, Delhi-52 and other members of his team for the presentable and timely execution of the monograph.

I would be happy if the treatise is able to attract the attention of scholars and students of Sanskrit grammar and the scholars who are interested in Indological Studies are arose their interest about a completely new study on the Sanskrit grammar and its history in Tibet.

Śiva-Caturdaśī
Santiniketan

Narendra Kumar Dash

SYSTEM OF TRANSLITERATION

a	अ	ā	आ
i	इ	ī	ई
u	उ	ū	ऊ
ṛ	ऋ	ḷ	ल
e	ए	ai	ऐ
o	ओ	au	औ
(a)m	अं	a(ḥ)	अः
ka	क	kha	ख
ga	ग	gha	घ
ṅa	ङ	ca	च
cha	छ	ja	ज
jha	झ	ña	ञ
ṭa	ट	ṭha	ठ
ḍa	ड	ḍha	ढ
ṇa	ण	ta	त
tha	थ	da	द
dha	ध	na	न
pa	प	pha	फ
ba	ब	bha	भ
ma	म	ya	य
ra	र	la	ल
va	व	śa	श
ṣa	ष	sa	स
ha	ह	kṣa	क्ष

ABBREVIATIONS

Aṣṭ	—	Aṣṭādhyāyī
BD	—	Bu-ston rin-chen grub; dkar-chag.
Bu.	—	Bu-ston rin-chen-grub.
C	—	Candragomin
CD	—	dkar-chag of Co-ne version of bstan-'gyur.
Co	—	Co-ne version of Tibetan canon.
CPS	—	Cāndra Pratyāhāra sūtra.
De	—	sde-dge version of bstan-'gyur.
DH	—	Dun Huang Ms.
GB	—	gnas-brgyad-kyi-'grel-pa.
GBCP	—	gnas-brgyad-chen-po'i-rtsa-ba.
Kā	—	Kātantra/Kalāpa.
Ko	–	Koṅ-sprul
Mah	—	Mahāvyutpatti
Ms.	—	Manuscript
Na	—	snar-thaṅ version of Tibetan canon.
N. cat. cat	—	New Catalogus Catalogorum
P	—	Pāṇini
PD	—	dkar-chag of the Peking version of bstan-'gyur
Pek	—	Peking version of bstan-'gyur
Prob	—	Probably
PS	—	Pāṇini's Pratyāhāra Sūtra.
Repr/repr.	—	Reprint

Sā	—	Sārasvata vyākaraṇa
SBBO	—	bgra-sbyor-bam-pa-gñis-pa
SD	—	sgra-tshad-pa rin-chen-rgyal-mtshan: dkar-chag.
Skt.	—	Sanskrit title of the work.
SMPD	—	Sgra'i-mam-par-dbye-ba-bstan-pa
Tā	—	Tāranātha
Tib.	—	Tibetan
Trans	—	Translation
Transl.	—	Translator

1

AN INTRODUCTION

Buddhism was established in Tibet during the reign of king *sroṅ-btsan-sgam-po* in early 7th century A.D.[1] The king belonged to the *yar-luṅ* dynasty, originally a clan of local chieftains in the *yar-luṅ* valley, south of the *gtsaṅ-po* river, which only briefly before his ascension had acquired the allegiance of several neighbouring clans, thus forming a confederation that would lead to the first more or less centralized authority over central Tibet. Under his rule the Tibetan State rose to sub power and extent of territory in Central Asia that is became an Empire. For more than two hundred years this dynasty managed to maintain the centralized authority over Tibet.

The first spread *(sṅa-dar)* of Buddhism in Tibet taken place during this period of Tibetan Empire, from early seventh century to mid-ninth century A.D.[2] Not all kings of the said dynasty were well disposed towards Buddhism, some favoured the local animistic cults generally indicated with the technical term *bon*,[3] the king's allegiance to either Buddhism or *bon* being a major political factor in the fluctuating play of power among the clans of Tibetan nobility.

A close study of the history of Tibet suggest that three kings have contributed most strongly to the propagation of Buddhism in Tibet. They were: *Sroṅ-btsan-sgam-po*, mentioned above, *khri-sroṅ-lde-btsan* (last quarter of 8th century A.D.), during whose reign Tibetan power reached its apogee, and *khri-gtsug-lde-btsan ral-pa-can* (1st half of 9th century A.D.). During the reign of the king *Khri-lde-sroṅ-btsan sad-na-legs*, the immediate predecessor at *khri-gtsug-Ide-btsan ral-pa-can*, Buddhism emerged as a significant political power for the first time in Tibet.[4]

The royal patronage of the newly arrived religion has greatly contributed to the development of Buddhism in Tibet. The adoption of Buddhism resulted in a huge process of trans cultural reception of a complex of cultural elements. In the wide range of cultural elements adopted in this process, for the present purpose the most relevant aspect is the Buddhist Literature. The translation of Buddhist scriptures in a large scale did commence in 8th century A.D., particularly after the founding of the first Tibetan monastery *bsam-yas* and the acceptance of Buddhism as state religion.[5] The creation of translation literature, consisting of several thousands of translation generally of high quality, reliable and consistent in terminology demanded that the Tibetan translators be thoroughly competent in and acquainted with the intricacies of Sanskrit language and literature. This led to the development of a tradition of Sanskrit linguistic studies within the Tibetan scholastic curriculum. Sanskrit studies covered such diverse topics as grammar, poetics, metrics and lexicography.

"The fifth descendant of *Lha-tho-tho-ri-gñan-btsan* was king *Sroṅ-btsan-sgam-po,* under whose great patronage Tibet was to receive the first initiation in the literary tradition. He sent *Thon-mi Sambhoṭa* and a party to India for the purpose of learning the Indian language. They learnt the Indian language and the Indian script under Devavidyāsimha and a Brāhmaṇa called *Lipidatta.* He also acquired the knowledge of grammar and literature and came a profoundly learned. *Thon-mi* devised suitable scripts for the Tibetan language. These were modelled on the Indian scripts known as *Lan-tsha* and *vartula.* Eight Tibetan grammars, modelled on Indian grammars, were also prepared by him." [Nagwang Nima and Lama chimpa, 1966; p. 400]. The view that Thon-mi had composed eight grammars, modelled on Indian grammar, needs some explanations. During 7th century A.D.; in India, the Aṣṭ of Pāṇini was popular. It may be logical to suggest that *Thon-mi* had prepared eight chapters (adhyāyas) of his grammar as like as Pāṇini's. However, at present we have only two chapters of this grammar viz; *trinśikā (sum-cu-pa)* and *Liṅgāvatāra* (rtags-'jug).

A central committee of translators, consisting of both Indian and Tibetan scholars, was formed and that was authorized to revise old and new translations to attain uniformity in terminology as well as translating techniques.[6] The committee is generally referred to as *bcom-Idan-'das-kyi-rin-lungs-kyi-'dun-sa.* A major contribution of this committee is a catalogue which is commonly called the *stod-thaṅ-Idon-dkar* or briefly *than-dkar [-mg] or Ladan-dkar (-ma)* catalogue; named after a place[7] where a good number of translations were done. The list is attributed to *Dpal-brtsegs* and *Nam-mkha'i-sñiṅ-po,* two translators who were active during the reign of *Khri-sroṅ-Ide-btsan,* so the first version of the catalogue can be dated to the second half of 8th or first quarter of 9th century A.D.[8] The catalogue as we know it now contains 736 titles, the majority of which being translations from Sanskrit. However, eight of the titles have been identified as translations from Chinese.[9]

It is evident from the extensive literature of translations from Sanskrit that was being produced at the time, that 8th and 9th century Tibetan scholars have occupied themselves with mastering the intricacies of Sanskrit grammar. The earliest Tibetan literature dealing with Sanskrit grammar is to be found in one of the two Tibetan canonical texts-collections, viz., *bka-'gyur* and *bstan-'gyur.* The second major source for relevant Tibetan literature is the unique find of early manuscripts for *Dun Huaṅg.*

During early phase we find two treatises that—wholly or partly deal with subjects of Sanskrit grammar. They are: (1) *bye-brag-tu-rtogs-byed-chen-po* or the *Mahāvyutpatti* (Mah.) and (2) *sgra-sbyor-bam-po-gñis-pa* (SBBP).

The work *bye-brag-tu-rtogs-byed-chen-po* which is generally famous as the Mahāvyutpatti contains a study on the declension of the noun *vṛkṣa* "tree" and a section on Sanskrit grammatical terms. The work mentioned is just immediate after this work is a commentary on a selection of words from the *Mahāvyupatti.*

The Mahāvyutpatti, a work on Lexicography was compiled by a group of Indian and Tibetan scholars during the reign of the Tibetan king *Khri-Ide-sroṅ-btsan-sad-na-legs* (799-815) and perhaps finished during the region of his successor *Khri-gtsug-Ide-btsan Ral-pa-can* (815-38).[10] The work was intended to standardize and codify the Tibetan terminology used to translate the corpus of Sanskrit Buddhist terms. Under the auspices of the mentioned kings the process also involved revision of earlier translations and checking of new translations by a central committee of translators, in order to attain uniformity in terminology and technique. The Mahāvyutpatti, as a handbook for translators, played a vaital role in the creation of the rich Indo-Tibetan translation literature which indeed uses a great many set patterns and phrases to translate Sanskrit.

The Mahāvyutpatti is a systematic Sanskrit-Tibetan dictionary, merely stating the Tibetan equivalents of Sanskrit words and phrases, mainly Buddhist terms, but also terms common to Indian literature and culture in general. Here we will find that no alphabetical or similar ordering has been adopted but the 9565 entries[11] are arranged on 283 meaning-categories, beginning with 'names of the Buddha' and ending with 'names of diseases'.[12]

The *sgra-sbyor-bam--po-gñis-pa* (SBBP) has 414 selected technical terms from the Mahāvyutpatti. It states the Sanskrit term and the Tibetan translation of the Sanskrit ones. Further it also comments and explains about the Tibetan translation chosen for the Sanskrit ones. Thus the SBBP gives an important insight into the techniques of translations used in the early period of formation of the Tibetan canonical literature.[13] The text is divided into two volumes. Hence the title *sgra-sbyor-bam-po-gñis-pa* (treatise on) the formation of words (consisting of) two volumes.

A close study suggests that the *SBBP* comments upon less than five percent of the entries in the Mahāvyutpatti. The order of the entries in the *SBBP*. is quite different from that in the Mahāvyutpatti. Although the *SBBP* in most cases incorporates the individual entries in the same section or meaning category as in the Mahāvyutpatti, generally the *SBBP* does not deal with all the entries found within that sense-category in the Mah. and the order of treatment of these sense-categories in the *SBBP* differs quite drastically from that in the Mah. In a few cases the *SBBP* comments upon a Sanskrit term that does not occur in the other work i.e. the Mah. Only two entries have been found in the *SBBP* that do not seem to occur in the *Mah*. in any form, viz. *o-sta-raga,* translated as *gnon-po* 'presser'[14] (*SBBP*. Pek. 32V5-6) and *ḍākinī,* Tibetan *mkha'-'gro-ma* (*SBBP*. Pek. 52V6-7). Some identifications are problematic, such as *cittasamprayukta sems-daṅ-mtshuṅs-par-idan-pa* (*SBBP*. Pek. 28V2-5) of which only the is mentioned as section heading in the *Mah.* 1921,[15] and *upavāsasthānin,* Tibetan *bsñen-gnas-la-ñe-bar-gnas-pa.*

Forms of Sanskrit grammatical analysis in the SBBP.

In the SBBP. several methods of commenting upon an entry are followed. In more than half of the entries the commentary explains and gives arguments for the Tibetan translation for particular entry in Tibetan terms only. We have left these out of consideration here, as they do not explicitly refer to Sanskrit grammatical analysis. however, on 203 of the entries[16] a commentary is given that contains some grammatical analysis of the Sanskrit term. In these cases a paraphrase or etymologizing description in Sanskrit usually precedes the translation and a further discussion of the term exclusively in Tibetan. These subsequent discussions often pertain to denotation and connotations of the term and its place in context of Buddhist ideas and beliefs. As they offer no material that is relevant to Sanskrit grammatical analysis, we have not taken these Tibetan parts of the *SBBP.* into account either. We have restricted only to the explanatory phases in Sanskrit, and their direct translations in Tibetan, especially those containing actual quotations or elements form grammatical treatises, as these phrase constitute explicit expressions of the Tibetan translators' competence in and application of Sanskrit indigenous grammar. The following types of grammatical analysis of the Sanskrit term will be distinguished here:

a. paraphrase
b. Separation of constituents of Sanskrit compound terms.
c. semantic isolation of suffixes.
d. morphological isolation of suffixes and,
e. isolation of verbal roots.

Paraphrase:

A common form of analysis occuring in the commentary on one hundred and eleven entries,[17] is in the form of a Sanskrit paraphrase which supplies an etymology of Sanskrit term. The etymologies given here are of varying value from grammatical point of view. Some are pious explanations of Sanṣkrit Buddhist terms, tending to popular etymology rather than giving a grammatically sound derivation.

For instance for the term *jina* (Tib. *rgyal-ba*); in a Buddhist context 'the conqueror of evil par excellence) i.e. (an epithet of Buddha)[18] SBBP. gives an etymologizing paraphrase in Sanskrit: jita pāpa-akuśala-dharma means 'he who has conquered the sinful and maleficent elements' a pious Buddhist interpretation of the term without actually going into the morphological and semantic derivations of *jina* from the root √*ji* 'to conquer,[19] with a suffix—'na' denoting agent of the action expressed by the root.

The Sanskrit paraphrases of fourteen entries in the SBBP. contain obvious forms of popular etymology.[20] An example of this is found in the commentary on the term *arhat*.[21] Two alternative paraphrases are given, firstly: *pūjām arhati iti arhan* means 'some is arhat because he deserves *(arhati)* praise'. Here a grammatically correct relation is indicated namely that *arhat* derives from the root√arh 'to deserve'.[22] The second paraphrase is: *kleśa-ari-hatavān arhan* means 'an *arhat* is someone who has defeated (*hata-*) his enemies (*ari*) namely the moral filements'. Here a grammatically incorrect etymology is suggested, deriving *arhat* from *ari* 'enemy' and *hata* 'defeated' (verbal adjective from root (√han). Remarkably the later explanation, not the former which is grammatically correct one, serves as basis for the accepted Tibetan translation of *arhat*, viz. *dgra-bcom-pa dgra>aṛi+ bcom-pa-(hata)* 'who has defeated (his) enemies'. The argument which is suggested in the SBBP. for preferring the later etymology is that the meaning or intention of the term is considered most important (implaying: more important than a morphologically sound derivation) as basis for the translation,[23] and apparently the later interpretation was considered to be a better expression of the full purport of the term *arhat* than the former.

Separation of constituents:

Another common form of analysis, accuring in eight seven of the entries,[24] consists of the separation of the constituent elements of compound Sanskrit terms, with a Tibetan translation for each of the constituents separately.

For example, the SBBP. commentary on the entry *āryāṣṭāṅgamārg(g)a,* 'the noble eightfold path'[25] as: *ā-ryā-ṣṭāṁ-ga-ma-rgga*[26]*-zhes bya-ba-ārya-ni-'phaqs-pa /aṣṭām-ga-ni-yan-lag-brgyad mārgga-ni-lam-ste /.* The term *āryāṣṭāṅgamārga* (consists of) *ārya* means 'noble', *aṣṭāṅga* means "eight branches' and *mārga* means 'path'.

In the twenty-six of the above mentioned cases[27] after separation of the constituents, one or more of the constituents of the Sanskrit term are glossed with one or more Sanskrit synonyms which are then translated into Tibetan. As per example in the commentary on *samyaksambuddha* 'the perfectly enlightened one,[28] we have *'samyak-sam-buddha-zhes-bya-ba-samyak-ni-yaṅ-dag-pa /sam-ni-sa-mantam-'am*[30] */ sam-pūrṇṇa-ste-ma-lus-pa'am-rdzogs-pa /buddha-ni-saṅs-rgyas-la*[31] *bya-ste /-* 'The term *samyaksambuddha* consists of *samyak* 'fully pure', *sam* (synonyms of which are) *samantam* or *sampurṇam* 'completely or perfectly' and *buddha* 'the awakened one'. Here we may mark that of the three constituents of the word, the first and third ones are immediately translated, but of the element *sam* two synonyms in Sanskrit are given, which are also translated into Tibetan.

Semantic isolation of suffixes:

In some cases the separation of constituent elements or the paraphrase of the entry involves the isolation of a suffix from its nominal or verbal basis. In twelve cases[32] after the isolation the suffix-morphme is not actually mentioned in the text, but it is represented by its semantic aspect i.e. a Sanskrit term or phrase expressing, the meaning or function of the suffix. As per example while comments on the word *maula* 'fundamental' or 'essential',[33] we find: *mau-la-zhes-bya-ba / mū-la-bhā-va-tvād-maula*[34] *-bya-ste-mu*[35] *-la-rtsa-ba'am /gzhi-*[36]*'am-dños /bha*[37]*-ba-ni-'byuṅ'ba'am'-gnas'-pa'ste,* "The term *maula* is explained as *mulebhāvatvād maulam* means 'something is called *maula* because it is originated *(bhāva)* in the root *(mūla).* Here the element *bhāva,* is not a morphological constituent of the entry *maula,* but it is a pre-presentation of the semantic value of the *taddhita* suffix—'a' that is affixed to the nominal base word *mūla,*[38] which results in the secondary nominal derivative *maula.*

The term *bhāva* is known as a technical term (t.t.) in Sanskrit grammar denoting the sense of certain secondary nominal suffixes.[39]

Although this and similar commentaries in the SBBP. of course indicated an awareness of the internal grammatical construction of Sanskrit words, they most often do not enter into the technical morphological details that are involved. As in the case of *maula* where the *vṛddhi*-substitution has been done for the initial syllable,[40] which is an integral part of the derivation procedure when affixing the *taddhita*-suffix in question, is not mentioned. Thus again we mark in the SBBP. an emphasis on the semantic rather than the morphological aspect of grammatical analysis.

Morphological isolation of suffixes:

A close study of the SBBP. shows that there are six instances[41] of the suffix-morpheme in isolation from its verbal or nominal base. For our practical purpose we have taken here only one instance like *bhagavat.*[42]

Bhagavat:[43] In the SBBP. the relevant part comments on this word as: *yaṅ-rnam-pa-gcig-tu-na-bha-ga-ni*[44]*-legs-pa-rnam-drug-gi-miṅ-ste /gzugs-daṅ- /grags-pa-daṅ- /dbaṅ-phyug-daṅ /dpal-daṅ- /śes-rab-daṅ- /brtson-pa-ste /'di-drug-gi-spyi-la-bya /bān-zhes-'byuṅ-ba-ni-bha-syā-sti*[45] *-ti-bha-ga-bān-zhes-ldan-par-bśad-de /* [pek. 4r 4-5]

Further, the word *Bhagavat*—stands for six good qualities like: beauty, fame, power, fortune, wisdom and endurance; and the portion—*vān* is interpreted as 'provided with':—*bhago'syāstī-ti bhagavān.* Here the secondary derivative noun *Bhagavat* is divided into the primary nominal base *bhaga* and the *taddhita* suffix which is referred to as -vān. This suffix-*Vān* is a nominative singular masculine form.[46]This is not the (base-) form which is commonly used by grammarians for this suffix when referred to in isolation.

The basic form of the suffix is *mat(up)*[49] which is applied to a nominal base to denote 'this is of him'. Under the circumstances the initial 'm-' of the suffix is changed to 'u' resulting in forms such as *Bhagavat*. However, the Kātantra system has the suffix 'vant(up) as the basic[49] form; but this occurs in the same sense as that of Pāṇini's.

The grammarian's phrase that indicates one of the semantic relation expressed by 'mat(up)' e.g. 'Vant(up)' viz., *tad-asya asti* corresponds to the paraphrase *bhago'sya asti* in the SBBP.[50]

The Tibetan translation of *Bhagavat* that is based on the interpretation, viz., *legs-Idan* 'provided with'/ 'possessing' the good, is not the only translation that SBBP discusses. In fact, this translation is restricted to the cases where the term *Bhagavat* refers to 'a wordly person' *('jig-rten-pa)*. However, when the term refers to Buddha, SBBP, prescribes the translation *bcom-ldan-'das* 'victoriously passed beyond',[51] which is based on a popular etymology that has several parallels in Buddhist literature.[52]

Isolation of Verbal roots:

Now we want to focus on the technical treatment of the bases to which the suffix are attached. The treatment of verbal bases in the SBBP. obtain contains an element of a strictly technical grammatical nature, namely a quotation in Sanskrit of a *dhātupāṭha* entry technically termed *dhātusūtra*. A *dhātupāṭha* is a lexicon consisting of an enumeration of semantically arranged verbal roots. The main Sanskrit grammatical systems have their own dhātupāṭhas.[53] A *dhātusūtra* consists of verbal root, combined with one or more *anubandha* followed by the sence expressed by the verbal root. A *dhātu-sūtra* may also contain more than one root, provided that they have the identical sense. A close study of the SBBP. enable us to identity forty Sanskrit phrases as *dhātusūtras*.[54]

The spelling of the transliterated Sanskrit in SBBP. is of varying quality. Even after correction of obvious scribal errors the form in which the verbal root is quoted in the *Sūtra* in the SBBP. in some cases differs considerably from that in the known *dhātupāṭhas*.[55] Here we must distinguish between the manuscript from Dun Huang (DH) and the later xylographic editions. In two cases a 11th century Ms. (DH) gives a more correct citation form of the roots (with anubandha) whereas the later block-print editions of 18th century A.D. have a corrupt form without any *anubandha*.56

When there is a discripancy, in general the form of the root as quoted in the SBBP. is more similar to the actual form of the root takes in the entry commented upon. We are not sure that whether the authors of the SBBP. (or later copyists) have intentionally changed the root forms and dropped the *anubandhas*. The function of the *anubandhas* lies strictly within the realm of technical word-derivation in grammar. They certainly make the root itself less readily recognizable for the Tibetan readers who were generally not acquainted with the function of the *anubandhas*. On the other hand, there were of course also easily liable mistakes by the later Tibetan scribal tradition.

In most cases it is quite possible to identify the dhātusūtras quoted in the SBBP. with an entry in one or more of the *dhātupāṭhas* known in the Indian traditions. In twenty-one cases the entry can be found in both the Pāṇinīya and Cāndra *dhātupāṭha*.[57] In twelve cases the quoted entry could be traced to the Pāṇinīya, but not to the Cāndra's.[58] However, in two cases it could be traced to the Cāndra's but is missing in the Pāṇinīya.[59] Finally in five cases no exactly corresponding entry could be found either in the Pāṇinīya or Cāndra dhātupāṭha.[60] It is not the fact that one *dhātupāṭha* is the source of all the forty *dhātusūtras* found in the SBBP. Our study suggests that the authors of the SBBP. may have consulted at least six *dhātupāṭhas* which were alive before 9th century A.D.[61] When comparing the sense-entries only, the Pāṇinīya dhātupāṭha has a phrase corresponding with that in the SBBP. in 37 cases, the Kātantra *dhātupāṭha*, the *Kāśakṛtsna dhātupāṭha* and the *Śākaṭāyana dhātupāṭha* in 33, the Jainendra dhātupāṭha in 31 and the Cāndra *dhātupāṭha* in 39 cases.[62] Thus, a single *dhātupāṭha* is not the source for the SBBP. This is quite possible because the SBBP was written by a group of scholars, at least fifty percent of whom were from India.63

Immediately after the—usually nominal—derivative of the root is isolated, the *dhātu-sūtra* is quoted, after which the semantic component of the sūtra is translated into Tibetan. We may argue that the main aim served by the inclusion of *dhātupāṭha* entries in the SBBP. by not so much in the morphological definition of the root, but in semantic component, which served as an important interpreting criterion for determining the Tibetan translation of the Sanskrit term commented upon. Thus, the Tibetan translation of the sense-entry of the root, either given separately, directly after the *dhātupāṭha* entry,or integrated into the following Tibetan commentary (Refer the SBBP. for details).

Conclusion

The sgra-sbyor-bam-po-gñis-pa (SBBP) (9th century) is a commentary on a selection of the entries in the Sanskrit Tibetan Lexicon the Mahāvyutpatti and it includes some kind of grammatical analysis of the Sanskrit term in its commentary on approximately two-hundred. In most cases the analysis is not of a grammatical nature, as when a Sanskrit paraphrase, often supplying an etymology of the term is given or when the constituent elements of a Sanskrit compound term are merely separated. In some other cases grammatical analysis a more technical nature is also found. Such as the isolation of suffix form its base occurs here in two forms: (i) only the semantics of the suffix are dealt with; (ii) the suffix-morpheme is actually isolated from the base. Again, an important element in the technical grammatical analysis of the Sanskrit contain included in the SBBP. is the quotation of *dhātusūtras,* forty cases of which have been quoted in the note—54.

NOTES AND REFERENCES

1. Though a tribal chief named Namri-*sroṅ btsan* (c. 570-620) was rulling over Tibet and exerted his power over the neighbouring tribes for unification, still the task was completed by his son *Sroṅ-btson-sgam-po* (c. 620-49), the first true unifier of Tibet. Cf; The Making of Modern Tibet, A. Tom Grunfeld, Oxford University Press, 1987, p. 32.
2. The King *Sroṅ-btsan-sgam-po* had married the princess of Han king and it was the influence of the Han princess upon her husband that the king adopted Buddhism, vide; Ibid, p. 33.
3. According to S.C. Das, the technical term *bon* signifies the "ancient religion of Tibet which was fetishism, demon worship, and propitiation by means of incantations. The word *Chos* which ordinarily means religion is used as the antithesis to *bon*. But now signifies the kind of Shamanism which was followed by Tibetans before the introduction of Buddhism and in certain parts still extant; of this there were three stages, namely—*'dsol-bon, 'khyar-bon* and *sgyur-bon*. The duration of the first extended from the time of *Gñah-khri Btsan-po* the first historical king of Tibet, down to the reign of king *Khri-sde*

Btsan-po; the second from the reign of king *gri gumb tsan-po* to the formal introduction of Buddhism under king *Sroṅ-btsan sgam-po;* and the third stage from king *Sroṅ-tsan's* time down to the time of Tsong-khapa." A Tibetan English Dictionary, S.C. Das, MLBD (Reprint) 1979, p. 879.

4. Refer, the Making of Modern Tibet, 1987, pp. 32 to 36 for details.
5. For over a century and a half Buddhism slowly permeated Tibetan Society in the struggle of its adherents to dominate their *bon* rivals. This feat was finally accomplished in the 8th century with the enthronement of *king khri sroṅ lde btan.* He was such an ardent Buddhist that he declared Buddhism the official state religion while following the Indian custom, he awarded states and sefs to the Buddhist monasteries and exempted them from taxes and coveres". Ibid, P. 33. Also refer, Tibet: A Political History, N.D. Shakabpa. Yale University, 1967, pp. 23-53.
6. Refer "Tibet: A Handbook", Bloomington, (Indiana University Asian Studies Research Institute Oriental Series-5), 1975, p. 202.
7. In some Dun Huang mss. the name of this place is spelled as *Lhan-dkar,* Refer, Les textes bouddhiques au temps du roi *khri-sroṅ-lde-btsan.* Contribution a la bibliographic du kanjur t du Tanjur, Journal Asiatique 241, M. lalou, 1953, pp. 315-16.
8. Refer, Ibid, pp. 315-16.
9. Refer, Indo-Tibetan Buddhism—Indian Buddhists and Their Tibetan Successors, D.L. Snell-grove, London, 1987, p. 441.
10. Refer, Indo-tibtische Studies, Die methden der tibetishen übersetzer, Untersucht in Hinblick auf die Bedeutung inrer ubersetzungen fur die Sanskritphilologie, N. Simonsson, Uppsala, 1957, pp. 212-213.
11. Refer the Mahāvyutpatti of Sakaki's edition.
12. The 283 meaning catagories are summed up in Sakaki's edition, part 1. pp. XXXIX-LVIII.
13. Refer 'A note on the knowledge of Indian grammar Among the Tibeta Translators of the Ninth century, N. Simonsson, Orientaila Succana 33-35, 1984-86, pp. 385-89.
14. We think the term intended here may be Sanskrit *auṣṭrika* 'coming form a Camel' or 'oil-miller', Refer to Sanskrit-English Dictionary, M. William, Madras, 1987, p. 240.
15. Sakaki wrongly attributes the Sanskrit form caitasika-dharmāh to mahāvyutpatti 1921, while actually this only pertains to Mah. 1922. Tibetan sems-las-byuṅ-ba'i-chos-rnams,Cf. Mah. Pek. GO 235 V 3-4.

16. The SBBP. suggests that the following entries are supplied some kind of grammatical analysis of the Sanskrit form: 1-8, 10-13, 15-18, 62, 79, 82, 88, 93-97, 100, 108-112, 115-117, 119, 123, 127, 129, 130, 132, 135, 136, 139-153, 156-76, 178, 179, 181, 182, 184, 193-94, 204, 212-16, 218-38, 241, 243-44, 252,-53, 258-59, 263-66, 271-75, 277-82, 285-87, 289-95, 302, 308-09, 311-20, 322-24, 328, 330, 332, 335, 338, 339, 346, 348, 351-52, 354-59, 361-74, 376-79, 382-83, 390-91, 402, 404, 406-09 and 413.
17. Refer the entries: 1, 2, 4, 7, 13, 16, 62, 88, 93-94, 96, 108, 110-11, 115, 117, 119, 123, 127, 129, 132, 141-53, 157, 161, 164, 169-70, 179, 181, 184, 204, 212, 218-237, 243-44, 252, 264-66, 273-74, 277, 281-82, 287, 291, 294-95, 302, 309, 313-14, 316, 319-20, 322, 328, 332, 335, 338-39, 348, 352, 354, 359, 361-64, 368-70, 371, 373, 374, 376, 377, 402, 404 and 409.
18. Cf; "jina, conquerer, standard epithet of a Buddha, so used in skt. 'May 12—Tib. *rgyal ba,* victorious; et passim. Teh word appears to be used of any head, or at least founder, of a religous sect"; Buddhist Hybrid Sanskrit Grammar and Dictionary Vol. 2; F. Edgerton, Yak University, 1953, p. 242.
19. DP. I/561.
20. Viz., Sl. nos.: 1. *buddha*, 2. *bhagavat*, 4. *arhat*, 13 *maharṣi*, 16. *krakutsunda*, 150. *aihipaśyika*, 212. *śamatha*, 295, *maṇḍala*, 309. *Śila*, 313. *poṣadha*, 319. yakṣa, 338. *pudgala*, 354. *airāvatī* and 369. *tuṣita*
21. Cf; SBBP. Pek 4V2-3, Co-ne 133 7-VI. Also Cf; "*arhant*, also (minadic) *arahant*, 9. V., the ideal personage in Hinayāna Buddhism, Fourth and last stage in religious development (...). In Mvy. 4. 5138, etymologically rendered Tib. dgra bcom pa, having conquered the enemy, as if ari plus root han." Buddhit Hybrid Sanskrit Grammar and Dictionary, Vol. 2; F. Eedgerton 1953, p. 67. The Middle India form arahant with the vowel '-a-' between 'r-' and '-h', being more similar to the combinaiton ari +han, may have played a role in the acceptance of this popular etymology.
22. DP. I/740.
23. This translaton principle is also mentioned in the introudction to the SBBP. Refer also Simonsson, 1957, pp. 245-46, and 269-70.
24. Refer entry nos. 3-6, 11, 13, 15-18, 62, 79, 82, 88, 95, 97, 100, 109, 112, 116, 130, 135-36, 139, 156, 159, 163, 165-76, 193-94, 212-13, 215-26, 235, 241, 253, 258-59, 263, 271, 275, 278-80, 285-86, 295, 308, 313-15, 317-18, 322-346, 351, 354-55, 357-58, 361, 365-67, 369, 372, 378-79, 382-83, 390-91, 406-408.

25. Refer *aṣṭāṅga,* F. Edgerton (Vol. 2) 1953, p. 81. Also refer, SBBP. Pek. 20r5, Co-ne 146r 3-4. It is to said that the text as found in a Peking edition is transilterated here.
26. Co-ne: mārgga.
27. Refer entry nos. 5, 16-17, 82, 95, 130, 135, 156, 163, 168, 193, 213, 215, 258-59, 263, 275, 308, 313, 246, 355, 358, 369, 406, and 498.
28. Refer, F. Edgerton, (Vol. 2), 1953, P582. Also refer the SBBP. Pek. 4V3-4, Co-ne 133VI.
29. Co-ne: *Samyak-sam-buddha-zhes-pa-sa-mya-ka-ni.*
30. Co-ne: *Sa-ma-nta-'am.*
31. Co-ne: *rgyas-pa-la.*
32. Refer entry nos. 110, 148, 150, 181-82, 282, 289-90, 320, 352, 371 and 409.
33. Refer, F. Edgerton (Vol. 2), 1953, p. 441.
34. Co-ne: *le-bha-ba-tvādme-la.*
35. Co-ne: *mu.*
36. Co-ne: *gzhi,* The reading *gzhi* 'basis' is preferable to Peking's *bzhi* 'four'.
37. Co-ne: *bha.*
38. The suffx 'a(ṇ)' is added to the word *mula* means 'root' by P. IV,1-83.
39. Cf; P. V, 1, 119 to 36 for instance. The t.t. *bhāva* could also be intended here, cf. P. IV, 3.53.
40. Refer; *taddhites-vacām-ādeḥ.* P. VII-1-17.
41. The six entries are : 1. *bhagavat* 'venerable', a standare epithet for Buddha. The Mahāvyutpatti-2, SBBP. Pek. 4r 4-8; Co-ne 133r 2-5; F. Edgerton (Vol. 2), 1953, p. 405; 2. *Śāstr* 'teacher', epither of Buddha; the Mahāvyutpatti-11; SBBP. Pek. 5V102, Co-ne 134r3; F. Edgerton (Vol. 2), 1953, p. 527; 3. *nirvedha-bhāgīva* 'belonging to or conducting to the four states of intellectual penetraton'; the Mahāvyutpatti-1211; SBBP. Pek. 12V8-13r2, Co-ne 140r 6-7; F. Edgerton (vol. 21, 1953, p. 305; 4. *Virūdhaka* name of one of the four world guardians in the Buddhist pantheon'; The Mahāvyutpatti-3148; SBBP. Pek. 1922-3, Co-ne 145r 4-5, F. Edgerton (Vol. 2), 1953, p. 498; 5. *dānamayapuṇyakriyāvastu* 'Abiding substance of meritorious deeds consisting of giving'. The Mahāvyutpatti-160; SBBP. Pek. 29V 3-4; Co-ne 153r 4-5, F. Edgerton (Vol. 2); 1953, p. 346 (under the title puṇyakriyāvastu); and 6. *Caturmahārājakāyika* 'belonging to group of the four Great kings i.e. the *lokapālas.* The Mahāvyutpatti-3078; SBBP. Pek. 34V 4-6, Co-ne 157r67; F. Edgerton (Vol. 2), 1953, p. 227 (under the title *catur-mahārājika*).

42. Refer note 41 above.
43. Refer note 42.
44. Co-ne: bha-ba-ni.
45. Co-ne: stī.
46. Refer P. V, 2, 94; P. VIII, 3, 1, Vārttika-2 and P. VIII, 3, 17.
47. Refer P. V, 2, 94.
48. Refer P. VIII, 2, 9.
49. Refer—*tadasyastīti mantvantvīn,* Kā II, 6, 15. It means the suffixs like *mant(u), Vant(u) (vin* and *in)* occur in the sense of 'this is of him'.
50. Refer, the SBBP.Pek. 4r 4-5 and Co-ne 133r 3-4.
51. Refer the Mahāvyutpatti-2 and also as in pali standard designation of the Buddha, Passim; Tib, e.g Mvy 2, *bcom-idan hdas,* victoriouslly passed beyond". F. Edgerton (Vol. 2), 1953, p. 405.
52. The etymology is also found e.g. in *Abhisa-mayālamkārāloka.*
53. For *dhātupāṭhas* in general please refer to: A concordance of Sanskrit Dhātupāṭhas, G.B. Palsule, Poona, 1955; and for the Pāṇinīya *dhātupāṭha* please refer: Pāṇini: A Survey of Research, G. Cardona, The Hague-Paris, 1976; pp. 161-64.
54. Refer:
    (1) *lokavid*: Mah-8; DH 3r5; *bi-da (-)d (a-) ña-na* Pek, 5r4, Co-133v7: *bid (a)-dzña-na* cf; P. *vida jñane* DP. 11/1064.
    (2) *Śastṛ*: Mah-11; DH 3r8 *Śa-su-a-nu-śiṣṭa'u* Pek. 5V1, Co. 134r3-śā-su-a-nu-śi-ṣto Cf. P. *śāsu anusiṣṭau* DP. II/1075.
    (3) *trāyin*: Mah-15; DH. 3V1: *tā-yi-ṛ-san-tāna-pā-la-nayo;* Pek. 5V2: *tā-yi-ni-santāna-pā-la-nayo;* Co: 134r4: *tā-yi-ni-santāna-pa-la-na-yoḥ.*
    Cf, P. *tāyṛ samtānapālanayoḥ* DP I/489.
    (4) *maharṣi*: Mah-17; DH. 3V2: *śi-ri-ga-to'u.*
    Pek. 5v4: *ṛ-ṣi-ga-to;* Co. 134r5: *ṛ-ṣi-ga-tau.* Cf. P. *ṛṣi gatau* DP. VI/1288.
    (5) Viśvabhuj: Mah-89; DH 3V5, Co-134r7; *bhu-dza-pa-la-na-a-bhya-ba-ha-ra-yo.* Pek. 5V8: *bhu-dza-pā-la-na-ma-bhya-ba-ha-ra-yo /*
    Cf; P. *bhuja pāpanabhyavahārayoḥ* DP VII/1455.
    (6) *kāśyapa:* Mah—93; DH—4r1: *kā-śṛ-dī-ba-to*
    Pek. 6r4, Co. 134V3: *kā-śya-dī-pa-to*
    Cf; P. *kāśṛ dīptau* DP. I/647.
    (7) *darśana bhūmi:* Mah—1144; DH 8V8: *'dṛ-śer-phre-kṣa-ṇa;* Pk, 12r7: *dṛ-śyar (?) pre-ksa-ṇa; Co. 139 b: dṛ-śyā (?) ta (?) pre-kṣa-ṇa.*
    Cf; P. *dṛśir prekṣaṇe* DP. I/988.

(8) *Vargacārin:* Mah—1007; DH. 9v6: *tsa-rya-'ga'-tya-rtha;* Pek. 13v1, Co. 140V5: *tsā-ra-ga-tya-rtha.* Cf; P. *Cara gatyarthāḥ* DP. I/559.

(9) *geya:* Mah-1268; Pek. 15v4: *kai-gai-śabda;* Co. 142v1: *gai-kai-śa-pda (bda),* Cf; P. kai-gai-śabd DP. I/916-17.

(10) *brahmacarya.* Mah-1280; Pek 16V2: *tsā-ra-ga-tau;* Co-134r4; *tsā-rya-ta-ra-ga-tau.* Cf; P. cara gathyarthāḥ DP I/559.

(11) *chinnaplautika:* Mah-1306; Pek. 18r5, Co. 144v2: *plum-ga-tau;* Cf; P. *pluṅ gatau* DP I/958.

(12) *viṣṇu:* Mah-3130; Pek. 18V2, Co. 144v6: *bi-ślo-byā-ptau;* Cf; P. *viṣḷ vyāptau* DP II/1095.

(13) *viṣṇu:* Mah-3130; Pek. 18V3: *bi-śra-(=s?)-pra-be-śa;* Co. 144V6: bi (–?) ś (a) *phra-be-śa; eb;* P. *Viśa praveśana* DP. VI/1425.

(14) *maheśvara:* Mah-3129; Pek. 18V4: *ī-śa-ai-śvatyāt* Co. 144V7: *i-śa-ai-sva-rya,* Cf; *ī-śa-aiśva-rye* DP II/1029.

(15) *māra:* Mah-3134; Pek. 18V5: *mṛṅ-ā-pra-ṇa-tyā-ge;* Co. 145r1: *mṛṅ-prāṇa-tyā-ge,* Cf; P. *mṛṅ prāṇatyāge* DP-VI/ 1404.

(16) *śakra:* Mah-3141; Pek. 18V5: *śakli-śa-ktau,* Co. 145e1: *śakḷ-śa-ktau,* cf; P. *śakḷ śaktau* DP V/1262.

(17) *indra:* Mah-3139; Pek. 18V7: *i-di-pa-ra-me-śvarye;* Co. 145r2: *i-di-pa-ra-me-śvaraya,* cf; P. *idi paramaiśvarye* DP 463.

(18) *Lokapāla:* Mah-3145; Pek 18V8, Co. 145r3: *pā-la-ra-kṣa-ṇa;* Cf; P. *Pāla rakṣaṇe* DP. X/1610.

(19) *viruḍhaka:* Mah-3148; Pek. 19r2: *ru-ha-dzan-ma-ni;* Co-145r5: *ru-ha-dza-nma-ni;* Cf; *Pruha bījajanmani prādurbhāve ca* DP 1/859.

(20) *pañcendriya:* Mah-976; Pek. 19v6, Co. 145v6: *i-di-pa-ra-me-śva-rya;* Cf; P.*idi paramaiś varye* DP. I/63.

(21) *dhyāna* cf; Mah-1477; Pek 20v1: *dhai-tsintā yam;* Co. 145r6: *dhyas-tsi-tta-yan.* Cf; P. *dhyāi cintyāyām* DP. I/ 908.

(22) *yoga:* Mah-1679; Pek-23r8, Co. 148v2; *yu-dzir-yo-ga;* cf; P. *yujir yoge* DP. VII/1445.

(23) *dauṣṭhulya:* Mah-2102; Pek. 28v5; *ṣṭha (ni?) -ga-ti-ni-bri-tau,* Co. 152v2: *ṣṭhā-na-ga-ti-ni-bṛ-tau;* cf; P. *ṣṭhā gatinivṛttau* DP. I/934.

(24) *dauṣṭhulya:* Mah-2102; Pek. 28v6: *la-ni-a-da-na;* Co. 152v2: *la-ni-ā-da-na;* Cf., P. *lā-ādān* DP. I/1058.

(25) *puṇya:* cf; mah-1699; Pek. 29v1: *puṇya-karmmani-śu-bhe;* Co. 153 r3: *puṇya-ka-rmma-ni-śu-bha;* cf; P. *puṇa karmaṇi subhe* DP. VI/1334.

(26) *mantra:* Mah-4237; Pek. 30v4, Co. 154r2: *mantre-gu-pti-bhā-ṣa-ṇe* cf; *Cmatri guptibhāṣMaṇe* 10/64.

(27) *vidyā:* Mah—4238; HD 23r1: *bi-du-dña-na* Pek. 30v5: *bi-dā-dzña-na;* Co. 154r3; *bid-dzña-na;* cf, P. *vida jñāne* DP. II/1064.

(28) maṇḍala: Mah-4240; DH 23r2: la-ni-a-da-na; Pek. 30v7: la-ni-sā-da-na; Co. 154r4: la-n-ā-da-na; cf; P. lā ādāne DP. I/1058.

(29) homa: Mah-4245; DH. 23r6: hu-da-ne; Pek. 31r3: hū-dā-ni Co. 154v1: hu-dā-ni. cf; P. hu dāne cf. hu dānādānayoḥ. DP. III/1083.

(30) śikṣāpada: Mah-7008; DH 23v1: śi-kṣa-ni-bid-dyo-pa-da-na; Pek. 31r8: śikṣa-ni-bi-dyo-pā-dā-nā. Co. 154v4: śi-kṣa-ni-bi-dyo-pā-dā-nā. cf; P. śikṣa vidyopādāne. DP I/605.

(31) śila: Mah-7009; Dh. 23v2: śī-la-sa-ma-do'u; Pek. 31v1, co. 154v4: śi-la-sa-mā-dhau; cf; P. śīla samādhau DP. I/523.

(32) samlekha: Mah-7012; DH. 23v5: li-kha-bi-li-kha-na; Pek. 31v4, Co. 154v7: li-kha-bi-le-kha-na cf; C.likha lekhane, VI/69 also cf; P. likha akṣaravinyāse DP. VI/1366.

(33) poṣaḍha: Mah-8678; DH. 23v7: dha-bu-ga-ti-śud-do'u; Pek. 31v6: dha-bu-ga-ti-śu-dhau; Co. 155r1: dha-ba-ga-ti-śu-ddhau; Cf; P. dhāvu gatiśuddhyoḥ DP. I/601.

(34) yakṣa: Mah-3218; Pek. 32r 6-7: yakṣa-pū-dza-ya-n(a); Co. 155r7: ya-kṣa-pū-dza-yin; Cf; P. yakṣa pūjāyām DP. X/1693.

(35) rāvaṇa: Mah-3378; Pek. 32r8: ru-ni-śa-pa-ta; Co. 155v1 ru-ni-śa-bda; Cf. P. ru śabde DP. II/1034.

(36) skanda: Mah-4761; Pek. 32V3: skandha-ga-ti-śo-śa-yo; Co. 155V2: ska-nad-ti-śo-ṣa-yo; cf;, P. skandir gatiśoṣaṇayoḥ. DP. I/979.

(37) dākiṇi: Mah x; Pek. 32V6. ba-ri-bi-ha-ya-si-ga-to. Co. 155V5: ḍi-bi-ha-ya-si-ga-to, cf. P. ḍiṅ vihāyasā gatau DP I/968.

(38) tuṣita: Mah-3081; Pek. 35r3, Co, 157r4: tu-ṣa-ni-pri-to; cf; P. tuṣa prītau DP. IV/1184.

(39) rasāyana: Mah-5776; Pek. 37r8, Co. 159V6: a-ya-ba-ya-ga-tau, cf; P. aya vaya paya maya caya taya ṇaya gatau DP. I/474-80.

(40) cāṇura: Mah-8213; Pek. 37v1-2: tsa-ṇa-śvaṇa-adā-na; Co. 159v7: tsa-ṇa-śra-ṇa-ā-dā-na; cf. P. caṇaśaṇa śraṇa dāne ca DP. I/796-798.

55. Refer not 63 above for detail.
56. The Dun Huang ms. has entry the trāyin ta-yi—ṛ (Refer note 63.3) and kāśyapa kā-śṛ (Refer note 63.6) both the root form with anubandha '-ṛ', while the later editions have more corrupt forms, viz., tā-yi and kā-śya respectively.
57. Refer note 63's sl. No. 1, 2, 4, 6, 7, 8, 12 to 18, 20, 22, 23, 27, 30, 31, 33 and 38.
58. Refer note 63's sl. no. s. 3, 5, 9, 11, 21, 24, 25, 28, 34, 35, 36, and 37.
59. Refer note 63's sl. nos. 26 and 32.
60. Refer note 63's sl. nos. 10, 19, 29, 39 and 40.
61. The S.K. systems of *dhātupāṭhas* are:
    (i) The dhātupāṭha of Pāṇinīya systm (5th century B.C.)
    (ii) The dhātupāṭha of Cāndra-vyākaraṇa by Candragomis (5th century A.D.)
    (iii) The *dhātupāṭha* of Kātantra system by Śavavarman (beforee 4th century A.D.) or Durgasimha (between 6th to 8th century A.D:)
    (iv) The dhātupāṭha of jainendra-vyākaraṇa by Devanandin (between 5th to 7th century A.D.)
    (v) The kāśakṛtsna dhātupāṭha by Cannavira-kavi or Kāśakṛtsni (after 6th century A.D.)
    (vi) The dhātupatha of Śākaṭāyana-vyākaraṇa of Pālyakirti (9th century A.D.)
62. Refer: A concordance of Sanskrit dhātupāṭha, G.B. Palsule, Poona, 1955.
63. Refer N. Simonsson (1957), pp. 241-244.

2

PĀṆINIAN SYSTEM OF SANSKRIT GRAMMAR

A Short history of Sanskrit Grammar:

The Indian grammarians are the first to analyse word—forms, to recognize the difference between root and suffix, to determine the functions of suffixes and on the whole, to elaborate a grammatical system so accurate and complete as to be unparalleled in any other country.[1] However, it is very difficult to assess the accurate, exact and consistent history of the evolution of Sanskrit grammar and to determine the date on the period of the origin and the development of the science of grammar in the remote past. If we will try to suggest any chronology, that chronology is liable to be conjectural or inferential and, therefore, hazardous, specially in the case of the very old treatises which are, often in all subjects, solely based on the internal evidence which is insufficient and sometimes vague. It may be, however, comparative Priority or posteriority may also ascertained directly and indirectly from the development of respective style and diction, of phraseology and language, if ideas and imageries, of various linguistic changes, the mention of earlier authors or works by name, important contemporary facts and the like. We can, therefore, at best, modestly infer the age or the different linguistic periods of grammatical studies pursued in several branches of Sanskrit literature within special reference to Vedic works of the most distant antiquity; and that again is only tentative and not decisive. Hence it is difficult to endeavour to construct a chronology and suggest a historical account, in detail, of the rise and progress of Sanskrit grammar. However, Pāṇini and Yāska, who must represent a stage of thought several centuries before the beginning of the Christian era, both refer to a number of grammatical authorities and their opinions. According to a statement in the Brāhmaṇas it was god Indra who first analyzed a speech utterance in terms of its parts.[2] Some scholars opine that the 'Aindra' school of grammarians were the originators of the Sanskrit grammar. Patañali refers to a tradition involving the futile attempt of Bṛhaṣpati to teach the language by enumerating its words and there meanings.[3] The earliest historical figure who dealt with linguistic study seems to be Śākalya, author of the *Padapāṭha* of the Ṛg-veda, who is mentioned by Pāṇini. According to Bhartṛhari, the sage Audumbarāyaṇa (also mentioned by Yāska) together with Varttākṣa, seems to have held views similar to the *sphota* theory.[4] A late tradition suggests that Sphoṭāyana, also mentioned by Pāṇini, is the founder of the *sphoṭa* theory.[5] Śākaṭāyana held the view that all words must be derived from verbal roots; some people consider him to be the author of the *Uṇādisūtras.* Gārgya and others held the view that not all nouns can be traced to verbal roots. But no authenticated works of any of these pre-Pāṇinian writers have come down to us, and it is difficult if not impossible to say which, if any, of Pāṇini's sūtras may have been taken from his predecessors.

Yāska and Pāṇini are two famous early writers on language. They belong to a period several years before Christ, possibly the fifth century B.C. Though Yāska generally considered to be earlier than Pāṇini, Paul Thieme opines that Yāska knew Pāṇini.[6] George Cardona thinks it is wise to leave the problem open.[7] Yāska's Nirukta provides the name for a discipline of etymology counted as separate from grammar, the discipline for which Pāṇini stands as the major seminal figure.[8]

History of Sanskrit grammar in Tibetan tradition:

In Tibet, as prescribed earlier some studies related to Sanskrit grammar began in the 7th century A.D.[9] Again, during the later part of 10th century A.D. when Buddhism reappeared in Tibet,[10] the Buddhist translation activities again were resumed. During this period two works of Sanskrit grammar were translated into Tibetan by *lha-bla-ma zhi-ba-'od* from Western Tibet and *Roṅ-zom chos-kyi-bzaṅ-po* and *chos-kyi-śes-rab,* from Eastern Tibet. Thus, according to our observations the actual studies on Sanskrit grammar began perhaps in the later part of 10th century A.D. These initial translations of the Sanskrit grammatical works are belong to the Kalāpa system of Sanskrit grammar.

During the earliest period, the translations of the Buddhist canonical works were a result of a cooperation between Tibetan and Indian scholars. This translation activities were going on upto the mid-fourteenth century a.d. and produced a huge corpus of translated Buddhist literature. In 14th century A.D the first exhaustive collections of these translations were made and assembled into the two Tibetan Buddhist canonical text collections known as the *bka'-'gyur* "Translations of the words of the Buddha" and the *bstan-'gyur* "Translations of the treatises".

The first completion of translations leading to the *bka'-'gyur* and *bstan-'gyur* collections was made in *snar-thaṅ* monastery by *dbus-pa blo-gsal byaṅ-chub-ye-śes,*[11] *bsod-nams-'od-zer* and *byaṅ-chub-'bum*. It is known from the history that the Mongolian ruler Buyantu Khan (1312-1320) had donated funds for this collection to the compiled. It is most likely that this oldest version of the Tibetan Canon consisted of manuscripts, not some printed form.[12] Though in the *bstan-'gyur* text-collection the main emphasis was on Buddhist Literature, still a considerable number of—not strictly Buddhist treatises-on linguistics, medicine, astronomy etc. were added to it.[13] The well known scholar *bu-ston rin-chen-grub* (1290-1364) was responsible for the first edition of the *bstan-'gyur*. His work consisted of eliminating duplicates, revising translations in order to attain uniformity of terms and classifying the material. A manuscript set of his redaction was kept in *zha-lu* monastery, but now feared lost.[14]

However two catalogues *(dkar-chag)* of this earliest redaction of *bstan'-gyur* have been preserved. One was written by *bu-ston rin-chen-grub* himself in 1335 A.D.,[15] the other by one of *bu-ston's* pupils, *sgra-tshad-pa rin-chen-rnam-rgyal* (1318-1388) in 1362 A.D.[16]

The later catalogue differs slightly from the former in ordering and contents. For our practical purpose we have consulted both the catalogues. Bu-ston's catalogue contains twenty-two titles of translated treatises on Sanskrit grammar[17] and the later catalogue contains the same twenty-two with slight variations and a minor difference in ordering and one more title that does not occur in the former.[18]

Towards the beginning of 15th century A.D. the muslim invasions of India and the subsequent eradication of Buddhism resulted in a dramatic reduction of the influx of Indian manuscripts in Tibet and put an end to the possibility of direct contact with Indian Buddhism in a living tradition. Nevertheless the interest in Sanskrit studies remained very much alive in Tibet and therefore, a number of translations of Sanskrit grammatical treatises were added to the *bstan-'gyur* at a later period. Now it may not be out of context to mention that twenty-four titles on Sanskrit grammar occuring in the eighteenth century editions of the *bstan-'gyur* are not mentioned in the fourteenth-century catalogues of the *zha-lu bstan-'gyur,* and these twenty-four titles are later additions. Thus, according to our study, a total of 47 Sanskrit grammatical treatises were translated into Tibetan during early 11th century A.D. to 18th century A.D.

These forty-seven titles on Sanskrit grammar are presented in this study. Out of these titles 19 titles belong to the *Cāndra* system of Sanskrit grammar. Thirteen treatises are affiliated to the kātantra/kalāpa system.[19] Four works follow the Pāṇini's system[20] and Sārasvata system is represented by three texts.[21] A grammatical treatise-cum-commentary-belonging to a system which seems to be wholly unknown in the history of Sanskrit literature and that seems to be based on mainly the Cāndra system called the *Manjuśri-śabda-lakṣaṇa,* can also be found in the later edition of the *bstan-'gyur.*[22] Two works are based on the Sanskrit grammatical philosophy[23] and finally four treatises cannot be convincingly attributed to one particular system of Sanskrit grammar.[24] In Indian traditional scholarship the famous grammar of Pāṇini (5th century B.C.) generally considered to be the most important indigenous system of Sanskrit grammar. It certainly is the most sophisticated tradition and in its long history—actually running up to the present century has seen the creation of an immense literature of commentaries and sub-commentaries. But, the extreme subtilty of the system made it difficult to serve as a text book for beginners or as a practical manual of the basic rules. This led to the creation of simpler grammatical systems to meet with those needs. The earliest of these practical manuals were produced in the Buddhist world.[25] The first we know it is entitled the *Kaumāralāṭa*[26] (before 2nd century B.C.) which has not been preserved in the Tibetan translation A recast of the Kaumāralāṭa is the grammar entitled *Kātantra* "Small manual" also known as Kaumāra and Kalāpa (or Kālāpa)[27] second half of 2nd century B.C.) attributed to Śarvavarman. Later, the *Candra* system of Sanskrit grammar, commonly called *Candra vyākaraṇa,* was composed by Candragomin[28] (prob. 400 A.D.)

The topical ordering of the *sūtras* is the chief characteristic feature of both *Kātantra* and Cāndra. Moreover, the description of Vedic peculiarities, as found in Pāṇini, which was quite redundant for the Buddhist, is absent in Kātanrta and Cādra. These two systems of Sanskrit grammar which are most popular grammars in the Buddhist traditions in general,[29] were generally current among the Buddhists in northern India[30] during the early middle ages. Thus, it stands to reason that, as the Tibetans mainly came into contact with the Buddhist tradition in northern India, *Kātantra* and *Cāndra* would be the grammatical systems they would become best acquainted with. That Cāndra and Kātantra were indeed the most popular systems for the study of Sanskrit grammar in the Tibetan scholarly world is corroborated by biographical literature on that period. It has been stated in the biography of *bu-ston Rin-Chen-grub* (1290-1364), written by his pupil *Rin-chen-rnam-rgyal* (1318-88) that his study of Sanskrit grammar centered principally around these two systems.[31] The same fact is also said about the grammatical education of *Dpaṅ Blo-gros-brtan-pa* (1276-1342) in the well-known histriography *Deb-ther-sṅon-po.*[32]

Pāṇinian tradition of grammar

Before going to discuss the works affiliated to the Pāṇinian system of Sanskrit grammar. We would like to present a short history regarding the life and work of Pāṇini, the founder of this system. According to the Indian tradition Pāṇini belonged to *śālatura namo grāmaḥ.* This Śālatura has been identified with the small town Lahur, situated four miles north-west of Ohind, ancient *Udbhāṇḍapur,* situated on the confluence of the rivers Kabul and Sindh, now in Pakistan.[33] Patañjali, in his *Mahābhāṣya* clearly mentions that *Śālātura* was not the *nivāsasthāna* of Pāṇini, but the *abhijana* only.[34] However, this suggestion of Patañjali indicates that Pāṇini left his native village and settle down somewhere else at least at the time of the composition of his work i.e. the Aṣṭādhyāyī.[35]

Pāṇini's Aṣṭ 'The Eight chaptered' is a very remarkable work providing a model for recent and contemporary work in descriptive linguistics that can stand with the best efforts of modern analysts. The eight chapters constitute a complete descriptive analytical grammar of the Sanskrit language comprising about four thousand *sūtras* preceded by a list of sounds by a list of sounds divided into fourteen groups, which are called the *śivasūtras, pratyāhāra sūtras* or *māheśvara sūtras.* In these sūtras the language is analyzed into verbal and nominal bases, so that the bases have come to be catalogued in two lists known as *dhātupāṭha*—the exhaustive lists of primitive verbal roots—and *gaṇapāṭha*-the selective lists of nouns, verbs, and so on for application in the rules. It is not clear whether one person worth all these different components of the fundamental Pāṇinian corpus. A further feature of Pāṇini's method in a set of metarules of *paribhāṣās*, which tells us in which order to apply the rules, where exceptions are to be made, and so forth. All of these components are, in any case, made the subject of a grand commentarial tradition extending to the present.[35]

Besides, some additional materials are ascribed to Pāṇini. Though tradition supports these the scholarship is less agreed on the authenticity of these ascriptions. Among them, one group of *sūtras*, the *Uṇādisūtras,* provides rules for introducing affixes after verbal roots to derive nominal bases. The authorship of these *Uṇādisūtras* is frequently attributed to Śākaṭāyana instead of Pāṇini, and some scholars have found them to date from a later period. It is likely that there is truth in all of these views, in other words, that the sūtras represent a development of analysis over a long period.[36]

Besides, the *Uṇādi sūtras,* a second set of ancillary sūtras are the *Phiṭsūtras,* which provide principles of accentuation. A feature of these rules is that accents are presupposed for nominal bases, from which the rules derive revisions of accentuation for the wholes of which those bases form a part. Because Pāṇini's rules contain none specifying accents for nominal bases, George Cardona reports that "it is clear that the *Phiṭsūtras* cannot be attributed to Pāṇini." In fact they are traditionally ascribed to

Sāntanava, a rather later writer. Still, there ar scholars who believe the *Phiṭsūtras* date from a pre-Pāṇinion period.[37]

The *liṅgānuśāsana* rules concern gender; they dictate how to determine the gender of linguistic items based on their structure and meaning. Although some scholars believe that the set of rules antedates Pāṇini and was known to him. Pāṇini in fact his own rules governing gender, which in some respects complement and in others contradict the rules in the *Liṅgānuśāsana.*[38]

The sūtras, further, are divided into six main groups: *samjña-sūtra* "technical terms"; *paribhāṣasūtra* "technical rules" or "meta rules", *vidhisūtras* "general rules", *niyama sūtras* "special rules", *atideśa-sūtras* "extention rules" and *adhikāra sūtras* 'governing rules'.[39]

Out of the six main categories of the sūtras, the *samjñā-sūtras* and the *paribhāṣāsūtras* have the common character that they do not operate independently. They have to be considered together with the sutras they server to interpret. First, *samjñā sūtras* and *panibhāṣā sūtras* are considered to effect at the place in the grammar where they are taught. Alternatively, they are considered to take effect at the time of *sūtras* requiring them.[40] The *vidhi sūtras* always are operated independently. Such as the sūtra: *iko yaṇ-aci* (p. VI-I-77) which is a *vidhi sūtra* is applied directly. The term *niyama* is very frequently used by grammarians in connection to a restrictive rule laid down with reference to the application of a grammatical rule generally on the strength of that rule, or a part of it, liable to became superfluous if the restriction has not been laid down.[41] *Atideśa* in Sanskrit grammar is a common feature which extends the scope of a rule beyond its normal bounds. Accordingly to Patañjali, in the Sanskrit grammar the governing sūtra exerts its influence in three ways : (i) generally by proceeding aheda in subsequent sūtras like the stream of a river, (ii) sometimes by jumps like a frog omitting a sūtra or more and (iii) rarely by proceeding backward with a lion's glance.[42]

Now we would like to present the history of Sanskrit grammar and story related to the life of Pāṇini which is known from the Tibetan traditions. Our survey on the historical data on the study of Sanskrit grammar in Tibet is based on a section of *Śes-bya-kun-khyab* composed by *Koṅ-sprual blo-gros-mtha'-yas* (1813-1899) [Ko.] and in two major Tibetan historiographical texts, viz., the *chos-'byuṅ* (religious histories) of *bu-ston-rin—chen-grub* (1290-1364) [Bu.] and *Tāranātha kun-dga'-sñiṅ-po* (1575?) [Tā.].[43]

Ko. describes the history of Sanskrit grammatical studies in two sections. The first section deals with the development of Sanskrit grammar studies among the upper world, the later section with that in the human world. The first of course containing exclusively material of a non-historical nature, while the later one typically consisting of a combination of historical and legendary or mythical themes.

Grammar in the upper world

According to Ko. the first grammar which was used in the world of upper world, was the Indra-vyākaraṇa As the name indicates, Indra, the king of the gods in both Hindu and Buddhist mythology, is considered to be the author of this treatise. Other names, both divine and human, are mentioned as well in connection with the transmission of the *Indra-vyākaraṇa* Bu. mentions Sarvajñadeva as the original author, but his work was lost.[44] Subsequently Indra wrote a new version, which he taught to Bṛhaṣpati Ko, however, descries that Bṛhaṣpati taught this system to India.[45] The statement of Ko's is similar to the Indian tradition. Patañjali, in his *Mahābhāṣya* opines that Bṛhaṣpati was the teacher of Indra viz., *Bṛhaṣpatir-indrāya divyam varṣasaḥasram pratipadoktānām śabdānām śabdapārāyaṇam provāca nāntam jagāma Bṛhaṣpatiś-ca pravaktā, indraś-cadhytā,* ... etc.[46] However, Tāranātha narrates a different story. According to him the grammar was translated from Indra to a brahmin named Indradhruva, contemporary of king Candanapāla.47 In the work "Pāṇini A survey of Research" (pp. 150-157), Cardona gives a survey of the various theories about the *Indra vyākaraṇa* that have been proposed by Indian and western scholars. Western Indologists now generally reject the claims to historicity of a grammar by Indra, and consider the *—vyākaraṇa* to a mythologized notion of one or more pre-pāṇinian grammatical traditions, or even to be purely mythical.

Grammar in the human world:

The second section of Ko.'s work is again sub-divided into six parts, dealing with five grammatical traditions, viz., *Pānini,*

Cāndra, Kāṭantra, Sārasvata and *Manjuśrī-vyākaraṇa* and finally a few remarks on some miscellaneous treatises subsidiary to these systems. It is to mark that the last two systems of Ko's are not at all mentioned by Bu. and Ta. But-Ston (1290 to 1364) is more or less contemporaneous with the author of the *Sārasvcta* grammar i.e. Anubhuti Svarūpācārya (thirteenth-fourtheenth century)48 and therefore, this system may not have reached in Tibet during Bu-ston's time. Again a Tibetan translation of the *Manjuśrī-Vyākaraṇa* for the first time was done by *zha-lu-lo-chen chos-skyoṅ-bzaṅ-po* (1441 to 1527/28) only in the later half of 15th century or first quarter of 16th century. Thus, there is reason that these two systems are absent in Bu-ston's work.

Now it is interesting to mark the silence of Tā. about the *Sārasvatavyākaraṇa,* as Tāranātha himself has made a partial translation of the sūtra text of this system.[49] It may be suggested in this connection that Tāranātha made the translation at a later date than his *chos-byuṅ* 'religious history', the date of composition of which is set at 1608A.D.[50]

According to common belief Lord *Śiva* was the tutelary deity of Pāṇini;[51] but in the Buddhist tradition this tutelary deity is identified variously. Bu-ston identifies this deity as *ma-hā-de-wa* i.e. Mahādeva;[52] Koṅ-spurl suggests that this deity is *'jig-rten-dbaṅ-po* (552.3) i.e. Lokendra or *'jig-rten-dbaṅ-phyugs* (552.6) i.e. Lokeśvara. However, Tāranātha opines that the non-Buddhsits mentain that Pāṇini;s tutelary deity was *dbaṅ-phyug* i.e. *Iśvara* (or *Śiva*), while Buddhists consider it to be *spyan-ras-gzigs* i.e. Avalokiteśvara, the later basing themselves on the prophecy on Pāṇini in the Mañjuśrimūlatantra. However, in the colophen of CH ^{II}/3 (Pek. 312 V2) Lokeśvara (Tib., jig-rten-dban-phyugs) has been mentioned as the tutelary deity).

In fact two prophecies about Pāṇini in Buddhist canonical literature are mentioned; one from the *Laṅkāvatārasūtra,* quoted by Bu. and Ko.: *sgra-byed-pa-pā-ṇi-ni* [Ko: ni'o][53] i.e. in the Sanskrit *Pāṇinin śabdanetāram* ...,[54] other from the Manjuśrīmūlatantra, mentioned by Ko. and quoted in full by Bu. and Ta. There we have:

bram-ze'i-khye'u-pā-ṇi-ni /
ṅes-par-ñan-thos-byaṅ-chub-tu /

ṅa-yis-luṅ-bstan-byas-pa-yin /
'jig-rten-dbaṅ-phyug-bdag-ñid-che /
de-yaṅ-de-yi-sṅags-kyis-'grub
[B: ... sṅags-'grub-bo]/[55]

This may be translated as: The Brahmin's son Pāṇini has been prophesied by me to attain the enlightenment of Srāvaka and he will also meditatively realize the noble lord of the world (Lokeśvara) by means of his (Lokeśvara's) *mantra*. (Obermiller translates on high Lord of the Universe).

Tāranātha mentions *yul-nub-phyogs-bhi-ru-ka'i-tshal* "the Bhirukhavana in the West (of India)" as the birth place of Pāṇini.[56] This idea of Tāranātha is also supported by Koṅ-sprul. However, Ko. mentions the place as: *'phags-yul-nub-phyogs-bhi-ru-ka'i-tshal.*[57] Bu-ston is silent about the birth place of Pāṇni. We may compare this view regarding the birth place of Pāṇini with the Indian's view that Pāṇini belonged to the village Śālātura (modern North-Western Frontier Province?). However, the consensus in modern Indology is that Pāṇini was indeed a North-Westerner.[58]

Now we would like to give the exact translation of Bu-ston's words regarding the author of the Aṣṭādhyāyī. He says: "Thereupon, when it had cased to exist, the Brāhmaṇa Pāṇini appeared. At first, being desirous to study grammar, he showed the lines of his hand to a fortune-teller who told him that he would not be possessed of the knowledge of grammar. Then he drew (the corresponding) line with a sharp knife,and set out in search of a teacher, but did not find any. Thereafter he propitiated Mahādeva who showed his countenance to him and asked:— what does thou desire? I wish to study grammar, —replied (Pāṇini). The god blessed him and simultaneously uttered the sounds 'A', 'I', 'U'. By this Pāṇini came to apprehend the whole of the grammatical science". (Obermiller, p. 167).

Regarding the total number of sūtras of the grammar of Pāṇini, the three sources agree with a some view that there are two thousand ślokas in total, viz., sgra'i-bstan-bcos-śu-logñis-stoṅ-yod-pa-zhig.[59] In this connection Tāranātha and koṅ-sprul specifically mention that these two thousand ślokas consist of a thousand grammatical sūtras and a thousand explanatory sūtras.60 This statement is similar to the observation of the

Chinese Buddhist pilgrim I-tsing (643-713), who describes Pāṇini's sūtras as a containing one thousand ślokas.61 Now it may be suggested that the Tibetan sources follow the observation of I-tsing. However, it has ben mentioned earlier that at present we have a little less than four thousand sūtras.

Both Bu-ston and Tāranātha are silent about the later literature in the Pāṇinian tradition. Koṅ-sprul, however, presents us a summary data on later Pāṇinian literature. He has mainly included titles that were popular in the Buddhist scholarly world, that is to say treatises that were suited to the needs of Buddhist readers. Subject wise ordering of the rules, restriction to the main rules and omission of the description of Vedic forms are the characteristics of the practical grammatical manuals that the Buddhists preferred. The first title of the late Pāṇinian works that Ko. mentions is the *Bhāṣāvṛtti* of Puruṣottamadeva Twelfth century A.D.).[62] Scholars opine that he was a Buddhist grammarian. However, according to our study he was brahmin by caste and adopted Buddhism in a later age.[63] No Tibetan translation of the text seems to be known but a complete palm-leaf Sanskrit manuscript of the *Bhāṣāvṛtti* has been noticed by Sāṅkṛtyāyana in the monastery in the central Tibet.[64]

The *Rupāvatāra* of the Celyonese Buddhist Dharmakīrti (between 10th to 12th century),[65] which is the earliest extant full recorded commentary on the *Aṣṭādhyāyī* and the *Prakriyākaumudī* of Rāmacandra (end of 14th century or beginning of 15th century A.D.),[66] which is the earliest *kaumudī* work which has been fully edited with a complete Sanskrit commentary, are the next two titles mentioned by Ko. Among these two works only the later has been translated into Tibetan.[67]

Finally Ko, mentions two names as Sanskrit grammarian: Śākaṭāyana and Kātyāyana. Śākaṭāyana is the name of a grammarian who is mentioned in the *Aṣṭādhyāyī* and consequently a pre-Pāṇinian grammarian.[68] However, the grammatical treatise entitled *Śākaṭāyanavyākaraṇa* is later than Pāṇini and it was composed by a Jain monk, perhaps Palyakīrti,[69] in 9th century A.D.[70]

Kātyāyana is traditionally considered to be the author of the approximately 4293 *vārttikas*.[71] The *vārttikas* are the limit or extend the scope of application and quality the interpretation of more than a quarter of Pāṇini's *sūtras*. They have ben incorporated in the *Mahābhāṣya* of Patañjali.[72] There is little evidence for determining Kātyāyana's date: approximations vary from the middle of 4th to middle of 3rd century B.C.[73]

The first and only Tibetan translation of a major work in the Pāṇinian tradition of Sanskrit grammar has been produced by "*dar ṅag-dbaṅ-phun-tshoqs-Ihun-grub* in the middle of 17th century A.D. (i.e. between 1658-60).[74] With the help from Balabhadra and Gokulanāha Mishra, two Pandits from Kurukṣetra (modern Harayana state), he translated the *Prakriyākaumudī* and as a separate text, Panini's sūtras as commented upon by Ramacandra.[75] During this period *rnam-gliṅ-pan-chen dkon-mchog-chos-grags* and an Indian scholar named Kṛṣnodaya translated the Pāṇinian *dhatupāṭha*.[76] Besides, a text entitled: *Prayogamukhavṛtti* was also translated into Tibetan; but the name of the translator is not known either from the text or from any other contemporary works.[77]

Thus, these four tests are the only Pāṇinian treatiss incorporated into the linguistic section of the Tibetan Buddhist canon, which are being studied separately in below:

CH/1: Title: *pā-ṇi-ni'i-byiṅs-kyi-mdo*
[Pek. 5913; Nā, 3905]
Pāṇini's sūtras on verbal roots.
Skt.: Pāṇini Dhātu-sūtra
Author: Bhīmasena
Translator/s: Kṛṣṇodaya and *dkon-mchog-chos-grags*.
Place: Potala
Date: Last part of the 17th century A.D.

This work is on the verbal roots (i.e. *dhātupāṭha*) containing a systematic enumeration of the primitive verbal bases and their denotations, belonging to the Pāṇinian system of grammar. Besides, some work on the *dhātupāṭhas*, belonging to the Cāndra and the Kātantra systems are also found in the Tibetan canons and those works will be discussed under CH III/9, 11 and 14; and CH. IV/11.

The Pāṇinian dhātupāṭha is the well known lexicon of the verbal roots in the Indian traditions. It is known from the history of Sanskrit grammar that the *dhātupāṭha* of this system was commented upon by Kṣirasvāmin (8th century A.D.) for the first time. Besides the *dhāturvṛtti* Kṣirasvāmin is credited with five more works related to Linguistics. In the 14th century A.D., a great Vedic scholar named Sāyana, had composed a work entitled the *Mādhavīya-Dhātuvṛtti.* This work deals with the verbal roots of Pāṇinian system. It is known from the said work that Bhīmasena had composed a scholarly work on this field;[78] but the original work is not available in India. Bhīmasena's speciality is that he gives the sense of the roots.[79] However, Bhīmasena was flourished some years before Sāyana i.e. in the early part of 14th century A.D.[80]

In the present text, the roots are grouped in ten major classes (gaṇas) that correspond to the ten different conjugations of present indicative and related tenses and moods. Within these classes various sub-classes *(antargaṇas)* with specific morphological or phonological properties may also be marked.[81]

It is known from the Colophon of the text that in the year of 1685 A.D. in the great palace Potala, the said work was translated by *dkon-mchog-chogs-grags* along with Paṇḍit Kṛṣṇodaya, an Indian Brahmin from Kurukṣetra.[82] The same source also mentions that the translator was inferior than Kṛṣṇodaya in knowledge.[83] However, the said work was completed by the grace of the Fifth Dalai Lama.

It has been mentioned that *dkon-mchog-chos-grags* had completed his translation under the auspices of Fifth Dalai Lama. The translator bears the title *rnam-gliṅ-pan-chen,*[84] 'great scholar of *rnam-gliṅ*'. Thus it is known to us that he flourished in a place named *rnam-rgyal-gliṅ* in the San district of *gtsaṅ* province. The translator has also composed a grammar for Tibetan language only viz., a commentary *sum-cu-pa* and *rtags-kyi-'jug-pa* entitled *legs-bśad-snaṅ-byed-nor-bu* to which he completed in 1683 A.D.[85]

Potala is of course the famous palace of the Dalai Lama on the *dmar-pa-ri* hill dominating Lhasa. Ekvall opines that "The great cliff of the Potala-part building and part mountain—is, without doubt, one of the wonders of Asia; but every lamasery, and even each small hermitage, reveals some of the same beauty of line and proportion that is characteristically Tibetan. The *Stūpa*, originally borrowed from India and called mchod-rten "offering base" has been modified into a distinctly Tibetan form;

and where ever it is found from Kashmir to Peking, it testifies by line and concept to the architectural bent, or even genius of the Tibetan: a dedication to the service of religion."[86] This was also the site of earlier places which however were superseded by the present structurer building work on the impressive palace as we know it now was started about 1645 A.D. and continued till 13 years after the death of Fifth Dalai Lama (1617 to 1682) and thus it was completed in the year 1695 A.D.[87]

The translations made in Potala palace viz., the *brda'-sprod-pa-dbyaṅs-can-gyi-mdo* and the *brda-sprod-pa'i-bstan-cos-chen-po-dbyaṅs-can-byā-ka-na'i-'grel-pa-rab-tu-bya-ba-gsal-ldan-zhes-bya-ba 'dar-lo-tsā-ba ṅag-dbaṅ-phun-tshogs-lhun-grub* (1665 A.D.) and the CH I/1 by *rnam-gliṅ-paṇ-chen-dkon-mchog-chos-grags* (1685 A.D.), were produced under the auspices of the fifth Dalai Lama.[88]

CH I/2: Title brda-sprod-pā-pā-ṇi-ni'ī-mdo
[Pek 5914; Nā, 3906; De. 4420]
"Sūtras of Pāṇini grammar"
Skt: Pāṇini-vyākaraṇa-Sūtra
Author: Pāṇini
Translator/s: Balabhadra and Ṅag-dbaṅ-phun-tshogs-lhuṅ-grub.
Place: Bras-spuṅs
Date: (17th century A.D.)

The text of the Pāṇinian system of grammar contains *sūtras* and *Vārttikas* concerning morphology, morphophonemics and semantics. The original sūtra text of Pāṇini is called Aṣṭādhyāyī and consists of eight chapters. Each chapter has four sub-chapters *(pāda)* and the *Aṣṭādhyāyī* has a little less than four thousand sūtras.

In the present translation the arrangement of the Sūtras is quite different from that in the Aṣṭādhyāyī. Here the order of the sūtras is identical with the *Prakriyā granthas.*[89] It is known from the colophon of the work that the Prakriyākaumudī of Rāmachandra. It is also to mark that the *uṇādi sūtras* have been included in this text, which are not part of the Aṣṭādhyāyī. Thus, the text has two special features: (i) the inclusion of the *Vārttikas* or a part of the *Vārttikas* and (ii) the inclusion of the *Uṇādi-*

sūtras. On the other hand we find here, just as in the *Prakriyā-Kaumudī,* that quite a number of Pāṇini Sūtras, mainly Vedic and accentual sūtras, have not influded in this text. Again, some sūtras that which appear in the Pk. also are not included in this text.

There are mainly four major sections of the text, dealing with *sandhi,* nouns, verbs and primary nominal derivations. The major sections are also subdivided into the following: Section one has Six sub-sections on technical terms, technical rules, *sandhi* of Vowels, hiatus, *sandhi* of consonants and *sandhi* of *visarga* and Second section is incorporated with twelve sub-sections on declension of masculine, feminine and neuter ending in vowels and consonants respectively, indeclinable, feminine-forming suffixes, case-semantics, nomical-compounds secondary nominal suffixes and reiteration. The section three has eighteen sub-sections on the ten conjugational classes, causatives, combination with verbal proportions, passives and the semantics of various tenses and moods. Lastly, the seciion four ideals with four sub-sections: to on various so-called *kṛt*-suffixes, the Uṇādi suffixes and the so called *kṛtya* suffixes.

For the life history of the translators please refer to CH V/2.

It is known from the colophon of the text that during the time of the Fifth Dalai Lama, the present work was translated at the great monastery *bras-spuṅs,*[90] one of the major centres of the *dge-lugs-pa* sect, situated some ten kilometres west of *Lhasa.* This monastery was founded in 1416[91] A.D. during the time of Fifth Dalai Lama there were seven thousand and seven hundred monks who resided there.[92] According to the book: "A cultural History of Tibet", in the twentieth century A.D. more than eight thousand monks were living in this monastery.[93] The colophone of this work suggests that the monastery is situated in the middle of the *dbus* province of Tibet.[94]

CH II/3

Title: *brda'-sprod-pa'i-bstan-bcos-chen-po-pā-ṇi-ni-byā-ka-ra-ṇa-gzhuṅ-'grel-gyi-go-don-cho-ga-dper-brjod-sogs-zin-bris-su-bkod-pa-legs-bśad-nor-bu-'dren-pa'i-śiṅ-rta (-zhes-bya-ba).*

"Chariot carrying jewels of aphorisms", consisting correct

interpretation, rules and examples on the basic text of the Pāṇinivyākaraṇa.
[Pek. 5915; Nā. 3907 and De. 4420].
Skt.: Pāninivyākaraṇa-samvandhi sūtrodāha-raṇādi viśiṣṭa-rathaviśeṣaḥ"
Author: Rāmacandra.
Translator/s" Balabhadra, Gokulanth Miśra and *ṅag-dbaṅ-phun-tshogs-lhuṅ-grub.*
Place: *bras-spuṅs*
Date: 1658 to 1660 A.D.

This is commentary on the basic text mentioned just above. We may shuffle suggest that this work is a true translation of the Pakriyā-Kaumudī of Rāmacandrācārya.

The present text does not correspond completely to the Sanskrit Text. Generally, the same basic rules (*sūtras* and *vārttikas*) seem to be commented upon, but here and there the commentary varies slightly, and sometimes the examples given are more different. In the colophon of the work it has been mentioned that the Prakriyākaumudī of Rāmacandra has been served as basis for the translation; but the sūtras of the *ākhyāta* section have been slightly extended by the learned scholars and some other sections that are easy to understand have been reduced.[95]

In size, this commentary is the most Voluminous treatise in the Tibetan carpus of Sanskrit grammatical literature.

The colophen of the text mentions that Fifth Dalai Lama had supplied all the necessary materials for this work and he also given many hundreds of gold and silver to the two Brahmin Pandits from Kurukṣetra to complete this work.[96] However, the work was completely translated in the year of 1660 A.D.[97] in the great monastery called *Bras-spuṅs.*[98]

CH II/4

Title: *rab-tu-sbyor-ba'i-sgo'i-gret-pa*
"Commentary of the prayogamukha" the gate of to usage language
[BD 18;S. 21, Pek. 2781, Nār. 3773, De. 4292]
Skt.: *prayogamukhavṛtti*

Author: Not mentioned [Navidharma in De. Tohoku]
Translator/s :
Place:
Date:

The work is a commentary in prose and it may be suggested that the basic work was in verse-form. The basic verses have not quoted separately in the work, but those have been incorporated into the body of the commentary i.e. *"rab-tu-sbyor-bai-sgo'i-grel-pa"*.

This text (the Tibetan translation of the commentary) is not complete and it comments only on two chapters dealing with syntax (Skt. *kāraka*; Tib. *byed-pa'i-tshing* and semantic case-relations (Skt. *samāsa;* Tib. *tshig-sdud*). An other text entitled *'brel-ba-grub-pa-zhes-bya-ba'i-rab-tu-byed-pa* (CH III/12) deals with the same subject with three more chapters. Thus we may opine that the basic work was in five chapters and the present work comments only on the first and second chapters[99] according to Pāṇinian tradition.

The original basic text of the commentary is not available at present. Therefore, it is not possible for us to study the work in any form. But we may safely suggest that there were one relations between the present work and the syntactical treatise entitled the *prayogamukhamaṇḍana,* known also by name *prayogaviveka* which has been attribute to the name Vararuci.[100] Abhyaṅkar suggests that Vararuci "who must of course, have been different from the grammarian Varaurci."[101]

In the beginning chapter of this teatise we find a sub-division of the six *Kārakas* into twenty-three types.[102] These twenty-three sub-types of the *Kārakas* are similar to the *upakārakas* of the great grammarian and philosopher Bhartṛhari.[103] The second chapter also contains a study on twenty-nine sub-types of the six *samāsas.*[104] A close study of the text suggests that the work is based on both Pāṇini and Cāndra systems of Sanskrit grammar. The technical terms which have been used in this text are similar to both the mentioned two systems.

As for example, the technical terms employed for the *Kārakas,* the case-relations, appear to be a mixture Pāṇinian and Cāndra technical terms (samjñā) viz., kartṛ and sampradāna being common to either system, while *karman* and *apādāna* are typical for Pāṇini; but *ādhāra* is typical for Cāndra which has been used as a *kāraka* term.

However, most of the technical terms are similar to Pāṇini's and the sub-types of the *kārakas* and *samāsas* are similar to that of the Bhartṛhari's. Therefore, we opine that the text belongs to Pāṇian system, of Sanskrit grammar.

Neither the colophon nor any other contemporary work mentions the name of the translator; the place of its translation and the date of the translation and therefor, it is not possible for us to mention anything about the said facts.

Notes and References:

1. Refer, Dash, N.K.; Puruṣottamadeva As Grammarian, Delhi, 1991, Page-1.
2. Refer the Kṛṣṇa Yajurveda V 1, 4, 7.
3. Refer the Mahābhāṣya on P. I-1-1.
4. The Vākyapadīya, II/347.
5. cf; the concluding verse of the sphotavāda by Nāgeśa Bhaṭṭa, see part two, summary, 45 on Sphoṭavāda.
6. Thieme Paul, Pāṇini and the Veda, Allahbad, 1935, pp. 23-24.
7. Cardona, G; Pāṇini: A Survey of Research, P. 273.
8. Refer, Encycopedia of Indian Philosophies, Vol. V, P. 14.
9. Refer, Tsepan W.D. Shakabpa, Tibet a Political History, Yale University Press, 1967, pp. 54 to 57.
10. Cf; Mimaki, K; Blo gsal grub. mtha chapitre IX (Vaibhāṣika) et XI (Yogācāra) edites et Chapitre XII (Madhyamika) edite et traduit, kyoto, 1982, pp. 12-15.
11. Cf; Ei-mer, H; Som results of recent Kānjur. research Sankt Augustin, 1983, for the historical developmnt of the *bka'-'gyur* and cf, Vogel, C, Vāgbhaṭa's Aṣṭāṅgahṛdaya-samhitā. The first five chapters of its Tibetan version. Editd and rendered into English with the original Sanskrit; Wiesbaden, 1965, pp. 24-30 for the historical development of the *bstan-'gyur*.
12. The Peking and *sde-dge* redactions of *bstan-'gyur* divide the section *mdo-'gret* "commentaries on *sūtras*" (which is one of two sections, the other being *rgyud'-grel* "Commentaries on the *trantras*") into fourteen subsections, amongst which we find *tshad-ma* 'logic', *sgra-rig-pa* 'linguistics', *gso-rig-pa* medicine, *bzo-rig-pa*, "arts and crafts', etc.

13. Cf; Ruegg, D.S., The life of Bu-ston rin-po-che with the Tibetan Text of the Bu-ston-mam-thar, Roma, 1966, pp. 25 to 30 and 32-35.
14. The *bstan-'gyur-gyi-dkar-chag-yid-bzhin-nor-bu-dbaṅ-gi-rgyal-po'i-phren-ba*. Cf. Ibid, P. 30, note 2 and A catalogue of the Tohoku collection of Tibetan works on Buddhism (nr. 5205), Toheku Univrsity, 1953.
15. The *bstan-bcos-'gyur-ro-'tshal-'gyi-dkar-chag-yid-bzhin-gyi-nor-bu-rin-po-che'i-za-ma-tog*, Cf.; Tohoku (no. 5249).
16. Ref, Ed. L. Chandra, 1965-1971, Vol. 26: 626-5 to 627-b; i.e. f. 113V5-114r 6, i.e. Section *mdo-'grel* Volume 'E (113) except the last two titles in 'E, viz. Smṛtijñānakīrti's *smra-sgo* root-text and auto-commentary that have not been included as they deal mainly with Tibetan grammar.
17. Ed. Chandra L; 1965-1971; Vol. 28: 559-4 to 558.4, i.e. f. 108r4-V4, i.e. Section mdo'-grel volume ŚE (117), again excluding the last two titles.
18. Cf; the CH III/ 1 to 19.
19. Cf; the CH IV/ 1 to 13.
20. Cf; the CH II/ 1 to 4.
21. Cf; the CH V/ 1 to 3.
22. Cf; the CH VI 1 to 2.
23. Cf; the CH VII / 3 and 4.
24. Cf. the CH VII / 1, 2, 5 and 6.
25. Refr, Lüders, H; Kātantra and Kaumāralāṭa, Sitzungsberichte Preuss. Akademied. Wissenschaften (Phil-hist. Klasse), Berlin, 1930 (reprint 1940), pp. 713-714.
26. Ibid.
27. Belvalkar S.K.; Systems of Sanskrit Grammar; Poona, 1915, pp. 81-91.
28. Ibid, pp. 57-62.
29. Cf; Renou, L; La Durghaṭavṛtti de Śaraṇadeva, traite grammatical en Sanskrit du xiie siecle, edite et traduit, Volume-1, Paris, 1940, pp. 39-40.
30. Refer, Keith, A.B.; A Hisory of Sanskrit Literature, Oxford, 1928, p. 431.
31. Cf; Ruegg, D.S.; The life of *bu-ston rin-po-che*, with the Tibetan text of the *bu ston rnam thar*, Roma, 1966, P. 81.
We have said earlier that while only Four works affiliated to the Pāṇini's systms have been translated itno Tibetan, Nineteen works of Cāndra system and Thirteen work of Kalāpa system have been translatd into the said language. This, of course,

proves that both Cāndra and Kalāpa or Kārantra systms were popular among Buddhists.

32. Cf; Roerich, G.N.; The Blue Annals, (in 2 vols.), Calcutta; 1949-1953; p. 786.
33. Refer, Dash, N.K.'s article, "Education in Ancint Asia as known from Panini", Asian Studies (Vol. 6, No. 4), Calcutta, 1980 pp. 1 and 2.
34. Ibid.
35. Ibid.
36. Refer, Coward, H.G. and Raja, K.K.'s (Ed.) Encyclopedia of Indian Philosophies, Vol.-V, Delhi, 1990, p. 14.
37. Ibid, pp. 14-15.
38. Ibid.
39. See Dash, N.K.; Puruṣottamadeva As Grammarian, Delhi, 1991, p. 9.
40. Ibid.
41. Ibid, p. 21.
42. Ibid, p. 23.
43. Full title: *dpal-gyi-byuṅ-gnas-dam-pa'i-chos-rin-po-che-'phags-pa'i-yul-du-ji-ltar-dar-ba'i-tshul-gsal-bar-ston-pa-dgos-'dod-kun-'byuṅ,* written in 1608, also cf; Vostrikov, A.I.; Tibetan Historical literature, [Translated from Russian by A.C. Gupta]; Calcutta, 1970, p. 158.
44. Refer, Obermiller, E; History of Buddhism *(Chos byaṅg)* by Bu-ston, 2 parts, Heidelbert, 1931-32; p. 166.
45. Cf. Chandra, L., Kongtrul's Encyclopaedia of Indo-Tibetan Cultur (Vol. 1) New Delh, 1970, p. 34.
46. The Mahābhāṣya *(Paśpaśāhnika),* Ed. Kielhorn, F; Bombay, 1880-1885; pp 5-6.
47. Cf; Schiefner, A. [Ed]; Tāranāthae de doctrinae Buddhicae in India propagatione narato, Petropolis, 1868, p. 53.
48. Belvalkar, S.K; Systems of Sanskrit grammar, Poona, 1915, p. 80.
49. The text entitled *Sarasvatī-vyākaraṇa* was translated into Tibetan by Tāranātha along with Kṛṣṇabhata (see CH V / 1 for details).
50. Cf; Vostrikov, 1970, p. 158.
51. According to the Kathāsaritsāgar, Pāṇini was a dull student compared to his batch mates. His teacher Varṣa was not happy with the progress of his student from Śālātura. The wife of Ṛṣi Varṣa took pity on the boy and advised him to go to Himālayas and worship lord Śiva to seek his blessings. The same text says that he was blessed by the Lord Śiva and wrote a new Grammar

(Vyākaraṇa Navam) i.e. *Aṣṭādhyāyī.*

52. Cf; Obermiller, E, History of Buddhism *(Chos byung)* by Bu-ston, part IInd. Heidelberg, 1932, p. 167.
53. Refer Bu; Chandra, L (Ed.), The collected works of Bu-ston, pt. 24, New Delhi, f. 862.3 and Refer Ko: Chandra, L; 1970 Vol. I; f. 552-4.
54. Cf; The Laṅkāvatāra sūtra Ed. Najio, B; Kyoto, 1923, p. 366, (veres-813).
55. cf. Chandra, L., (1965-1971), Vol. 24, f. 863. 4-5.
56. cf; Schiefner, A, 1868, p. 42.
57. cf; Chandra, L. 1970, Vol. I, f. 552.4.
58. "According to tradition, Pāṇini came from Śālātura in the north-west of the subcontinent. This is reasonable and to my knowledge, only one scholar has seriously ... etc."
    Cardona, G; Pāṇini: A Survey of Research; new Delhi, 1976, p. 268.
59. cf; Chandra, L; (1965-1971) vol. 24, f. 863.5. However, Obermiller translates that there were 2000 rules, which seems to be wrong (see Obermiller, P. 167).
60. cf; *sgra-sbyor-ba'i-mdo-śloka-stoṅ-daṅ / bye-brag phyed-pa-i-mdo-śloka stoṅ-ste-ñis-ston-yod-pa-cig* (Tā). According to the other source i.e. Ko: *ślo-ka-stoṅ-daṅ /bye-brag-'byed-pa'i-mdo-śloka-stoṅ-yod-pa.*
    Ref Schiefner, A; 1968, p. 43 for the former and Chandra, L. 1970, vol. 1; f. 552.7 for the later.
61. Refer, Takakusu, J (trns); A Record of the Buddhist Religion as practised in India and the Malay Archipelago, by I-Tsing, Oxford, 1896, p. 172.
62. See, Dash, N.K.; Puruṣottamadeva As Grammarian, Delhi, 1991, p. 66.
64. Cf; Sāṅkṛtyāyana, R; Sanskrit Palm-leaf Mss. in Tibet; JBORS XXI, 1, 1935, p. 35, no. 90.
65. See, Cardona, G; 1976, p. 285.
66. Ibid, p. 286.
67. Cf; CH II/ 3.
68. Se, Cardona, G; 1976, pp. 146-48 and 149.
69. Cf; Ibid, p. 149 and also cf; Scharfe, H; Grammatical literature; A History of Indian literature, Vol. V, Fase, 2 [ed. J. Gonda] Wiesbaden, 1976, p. 169.
70. Ibid; and also Cf;
    "Pālyakīrti-another name of Śākaṭāyana, the author of Śākaṭāyana Vyākaraṇa, along with his own commentary Amoghavṛtti. He belonged to the Yāpanīya Jain Saṅgha and

lived around 867 to 910 A.D. ... ", Abhyaṅkar, K.V.; and Shukla, J.M., 1986, p. 250.

71. Ibid, 1986, pp. 349-50.
72. cf; Cardona, G., 1976, pp. 244, 247, 250-53.
73. Ibid, pp. 267-68.
74. Cf; CH II / 3.
75. Cf; CH II / 2.
76. Cf; CH II / 1.
77. Cf; CH II / 4.
78. Cf; Blvelkar, S.K., 1915, p. 44.
79. Ref. Abhyankar, K.V., and Shukla, J.M.; 1986, p. 295.
80. Ibid.
81. For a descripton of the contents of the *gaṇas* and *antargaṇas,* cf; Palsule, G.B; The Sanskrit dhātupāṭhas—A critical study, Poona, 1961, pp. 27-36. and Cardona, G; Delh, 1988, pp. 116-39.
82. cf; *// zhes-pa-rgya-gar-nub-phyogs-ku-ru-kse-tra'i-paṇḍita-kṛṣṇo-da-ya-zhes-bram-ze-gtsaṅ-ma'i-rigs-su-gyur-pa-de-ñid-kyi-druṅ-du / kun-mkhyen-rgyal-ba'i-dbaṅ-po-thams-cad-mkhyen-pa-chen-po'i-bka'-drin-gyis-ñe-bar-*[two syllables illegible]*...'i-bká-baṅs-kyi-tha-śal-dkon-mchog-chos-grags-kyis-rab-byuṅ-bcu-drug-pa-śiṅ-glaṅ-gi-lor-pho-braṅ-chen-po-po-ta-lar / raṅ-gis-ji-bzhin-dpyod-nus-pa-dka'-yaṅ-paṇḍi-ta'i-gsuṅ-rgyun-la-brten-nas-cha-tsam-bsgyur-ba'o //* Pek. 358r 2-4:
83. cf; Ibid.
84. cf; Ibid.
85. Cf; Tillmans, T.J.F; and Herforth, D.D.; Agents and Actions in classical Tibetan. The Indigenous Grammarians on Bdag and Gzan and Bya byed las gsum, Wien, 1989, 9, P. 31. It is to mark here that G. Tucci in the work: Tibetan Painted scrolls, [Roma, 1949] mentions the title as " *sna-byed-nor-bu.*
86. cf; Shakabpa, T.W.D.; Tibet A Political History, Yale Uniersity Press, 1967, p. 40.
87. Ibid, p. 128.
88. See the colophons of Ch II / 1, Ch II / 2 and CH II / 3.
89. Refer; Dash, N.K; 1991, pp. 6-7.
90. *// de-ltar-phags-pa-'jig-rten-dbaṅ-phyug-gis-slob-dpon-chen-po-Pā-ṇi-ni-las-dṅos-su-stsal-pa /brda'-sprod-kun-gyi-pyi-mo-Pā-ṇi-ni-byā-ka-ra-ṇa'i-mdo-'di-ni-raṅ-cag-bsil-ldan-pa-rnams-kyi-mtshuṅs-pa-med-pa-'i skyabs -daṅ- / mgon-daṅ / dpuṅ-gñen-dam-pa"phags-pa-phyag-na-padma-sum-ldan-rdo-rje-'dzin-pa'i-skur-bzheṅs-pa-rgyal-ba'i-dbaṅ-po-thams-cad-mkhyen-pa-chen-pos-mthun-pa'i-yo-byad-thams-cad-'bad-*

med-du-stsal-te /'di-ltar-sgyur-cig-ces-bka'i-gnaṅ-ba-thob-par-brten-'phags-yul-nub-phyogs-ku-ru-kṣe-trar-bram-ze'i-rigs-las-'khruṅs-pa-ma-hā-paṇḍita-ba-la-bha-dra-daṅ- / skyabs-mchog-rgyal-dbaṅ-chen-po'i-mñam-pa-med-pai'i-bká-drin-las / brda-sprod-pai-riṅ-lugs-la-cuṅ-zad-tsam-sbyaṅs-pa-bodkyi-lo-tsā-ba-'dar-pa-ṅag-dbaṅ-phun-tshogs-lhun-grub-kyis /bod-yul-dbus-kyi-ste-ba-chos-gra-chen-po-dpal-ldan-'bras-spuṅs-su-slob-dbon-chen-bp-rā ma-tsandras-mdzad-pa'i-'grel-bar-brten-nas-bsgyur-ba'o /[Pek. 312 V 2-6]

91. Refer; Snellgrove, D.L. and Richardson, H.E.; A Cultural History of Tibet, London, 1968, p. 182.
92. Snellgrove, D.L. and Richardson, H.E., 1968, pp. 237-38.
93. Ibid.
94. Refer note—90 above.
95. cf: *slob-dpon-chen-po-rā-ma-tsandras-mdzad-pa'i-grel-pa-pra-kri-yā-ste-rab-tu-bye-ba-zhes-pa-gzhir-gzhag /kun-bśad-sogs-rtsa-bsgrub-ky-mchan-bu-zhib-par-btab-yod-chos-ga-rtogs-dka'-ba-rnams-la-slob-dpon-mkhas-pa'i-gsuṅ-rgyun-gyis-zur-brgyan-te-cuṅ-zad-rgyas-par-byas / rtogs-sla-ba-rnams-ñuṅ-ṅur-byas-te* / Pek. 265V 1-2.
96. Ref. Pek. 265 r2-v4 and Co. 452v2—453r3 fro the Colophon.
97. The translation was begun on an auspicious day in the waxing moon in the month chu-stod (Pūrvāṣāḍhā i.e. the Sixth Hor month) inthe earth male-dog year called *Rnam-phyaṅ* (i.e. 1658) ten cycles of sixty years and thirty-one single years, the year of death of *me-mkha-rgya-mtsho*, When I had reached the age of twenty-five. This translation was finished on the auspitious day of *Pa-śe*, the third thursday of the waning period in the *Nag-pa* month in the year iron-mouse called *kun-ldan* (i.e. 1660 A.D.) Refer the Colophon: */ me-mkha-rgya-mtsho-la-'das-lo-drug-cu-skor-bcu-daṅ-ñag-sum-cu-rtsa-gcig-bsre-ba-rnam-'phyaṅ-zhes-pa-sa-pho-khyi-lo-ñer-lṅar-sleb-pa-chu-stod-zla-bai'i-yar-tshes-dge-bar-'go-brtsams / kun-ldan-zhes-pa-lcags-byi-nag-pa-zla-ba'i-dmar-phyogs-kyi—rgyal-ba-gsum-pa-śe'i-'grub-sbyor-gyi-dus-dge-bar-chos-grwa-chen-po-dpal-ldan-'bras-spuṅs-kyi-raṅ-śag-rgyud-steṅ-spyil-por-sbyar-ba-'dis-kyaṅ-bstan-pa-daṅ-sems-can-yoṅs-la-phan-par-gyur-cig* / [Pek. 265 v. 4]

    Also refer Shakabpa, T.W.D.; 1967, pp. 15-17 for the calculation of Tibetan date.
98. Refer the Colophon above (note-97).
99. cf; concluding phrase: *de-ni-lṅa-pa-las-gñis-par-'gyur-bar-smras-pa-ste* /Pek. 245V6.

Again the missing three sections dealt with secondary nominal derivatives (Skt. *taddhita,* Tib. *de-la-phan-pa*); verbal forms (Skt. *tiṅganta;* Tib *ti-ṅa'i'rkyen-can*) and primary nominal derivatives (Skt. *kṛt* Tib. *byed-pa'i-rkyen-can),* cf; Pek. 241 7-V1.

100. Abhyankar, K.V. and Shukla, J.M., 1986, p. 270.

101. Ibid.

102. Chapter one of the text contains the following 23 sub-types of the Six *kārakas:*
bved-pa-po [*kartṛ* 5 types]
las [*karman* 7 types], *beyed-pa* [karaṇa 2 types], *yaṅ-dag-par-sbyin-pa* [*sampradāna* 3 types]
gaṅ-las-'oṅs-pa [*apādāna* 2 types]
gnas-gzhi [*adhikaraṇa* 4 types]
Please refer Pek. 238V2-241V2 for details.

103. Refer the Sādhana samuddeśa in the 3rd chapter of the Vākyapadīya of Bhartṛhaṅ.

104. Chapter two is incorporated with the following 29 sub-types of the *samāsas:*

d'i-skyes-bu	[*tatpuruṣa*	8 types]
les-'dzin-pa	[*karmadhāraya*	6 types]
'bru-maṅ-po	[*bahurvrīhi*	7 types]
ba-gñis-pa	[*dvigu*	2 types]
Zlas-dbye-ba	[*dvandva*	4 types]
Zad-pur-mi-'gyur-ba	[*avyayibhāva*	2 types]

Ref Pek. 241v2 to 245v6 for details.

3

CĀNDRA SYSTEM OF SANSKRIT GRAMMAR

History of Cāndra system (Indian tradition)

The period between the time of Patañjali (150 B.C.) and that of Bhartṛhari (5th century A.D.), is credited with a number of the other systems of Sanskrit grammar other than Pāṇini's. The other systems include the Digambara school of Jainendra, the Buddhist Cāndra school and the Kātantra or Kālapa tradition.

Buddhist Grammar dates at least from Candragomin, to whom the *Cāndrasūtras* are ascribed, and who appears to have lived about Bhartṛhari's time, in the fourth or fifth century A.D. The work of Candragomin was meant as an improvement on that of Pāṇini, Kātyāyana, and Patañjali, mainly in the way of greater brevity and precision. The Pāṇiniya sūtras which are meant for vedic accents and grammar, have been omitted by Candragomin but he includes some vedic roots in his Dhātupāṭha. There are thirteen *pratyāhāra* sūtras in the grammar as he reads the sūtras *ha-ya-va-raṭ* (P.S.5) and *laṇ* (P.S.6) of Pāṇini as a single one i.e *ha-ya-va-ra-laṇ* (C.P.S.5). It is interesting to mark that in many cases, the sūtras of Pāṇini are recast simply for the sake of securing facility of pronunciation. For example, Pāṇini's *sūtra anekāl-śit-sarvasya* (P.I.I.55) has been re-arranged by Candragomin as: *śid-anekāl sarvasya* (C.I.-1-12). The total number of the sūtras in *Cāndra vyākaraṇa* are 3,100 as against near about 4000 of Pāṇini. The grammar of Candragomin cosists of six chapters of four *padas* (sub-chapter) each. There are also accessory lits: a *Dhātupāṭha, Liṅgānuśāsana, Gaṇapāṭha Upasargavṛtti,* and *Varṇasūtras,* and a commentary written by Candragomin, fragments of which have come down to us. This grammar seems to have been popular among the Buddhists, was translated into Tibetan, and was circulated throughout Buddhist Lands. It is still studied in Tibet, though not in Śrī Laṅkā, where it was later superseded by Kāśyapa's *Bālāvabodha* (ca. 1200).[1]

History of Cāndra system (Tibetan tradition):

Koṅ-sprul blo-gros-mtha'-yas narrates the history of *Cāndravyākaraṇa* just after Pāṇini. Besides, both Bu-ston and Tāranātha also contain elaborate biographical notices on Candragomin. These three identify the grammarian with the Buddhist author Candragomin, who composed many *stotras* and tāntric manuals found in Buddhist canon.

It has been mentioned that the grammarian Candragomin was flourished before Bhartṛhari, the author of the Vākyapadīya. However, the Buddhist Candragomin is placed in the later three quarters of the seventh century A.D.[2] This difference seems to exclude the possibility of identifying these two authors.[3]

The great Tibetologist Bu-ston states that Candragomin was born in eastern India i.e. in Bengal. He, however, does not mentions more details about the birth place of this great grammarian from Bengal.[4] Tāranātha and Koṅ-sprul opine that Varendra was the birth place of the grammarian Candragomin.[5] Varendra or Varendri may be identified as the modern Rajashahi District of Bangladesh.[6] The grammarian's spiritual association with Lokeśvara and Tārā is mentioned by most of the Tibetologists. He is also described as a productive author who is supposed to have written 432 works. These 432 works include 103 *stotras*, 108 Buddhist treatises, 108 Secular treatises and 108 treatises on arts.[7] Indeed, quite a number of *stotras* in Tibetan canon are attributed to Candragomin. In these *stotras* his particular devotion to Lokeśvara and Tāra is apparent.

Koṅ-sprul remarks that Candragomin had composed his treatise on grammar after studying the *Mahābhāṣya* of Patañjali in southern Indian tradition. He had found the *Mahābhāṣya* to be verbose yet small in meaning, repetative yet incomplete'.[8] This remark of Candragomin seems to be harsh. However, Tāranātha opines that this remark is an insult to the author of the *Mahābhāṣya*.[9] Actually, the three qualities of *Cāndravyākaraṇa* as: short, clear and complete is known from the opening stanza. The author himself writes at the beginning of his treatise as:

> *siddham praṇamya sarvajñam sarvījam jagato gurum /*
> *laghu-vispaṣṭa-sampūrṇam-ucyate śabdalakṣaṇam //*[10]

It means: after (I) have paid homage to the perfect omniscient teacher of the world who is beneficient to all, a description of language that is short, clear and complete (will) be expounded (by me).

According to *koṅ-sprul* the *Cāndravyākaraṇa* has seven hundred *ślokas* which form twenty-four chapters. However, the present edition of this treatise has six chapters with four sub-chapters in each and contains 3100 sūtras. Tāranātha gives no reference about the size of the work. Bu-ston, on the other hand, mentions that there are thirty-two chapters and seven hundred verses in the *Cāndra-vyākaraṇa.*[11] There are indication that the said grammar originally was written in eight volumes presumably of four *padas* in each, which would amount to thirty two chapters. The seventh book (on Vedic *sūtras*) and the eighth (on accents) are missing now, supposedly as these sections were less relevant for the Buddhists.[12] It is interesting to note that Bu, the earliest of our sources, still knew of a version consisting of eight chapters. In the catalogue of Bu-ston's first redaction of the *bstan'-gyur* there is no specification of the size of the *Cāndra-vyākaraṇa* that was included in this earliest *bstan-'gyur.*[13] Consequently it is not possible to tell whether Bu. merely knew of a version in eight books, or the text actually still was—or had recently been—current in eight books.[14]

Again, while Tā. is silent about any subsidiary treatises in the *Cāndra* system, both Bu. and Ko. mention quite a few treatises from the elaborate supplementary *Cāndra* literature.[15] They mention a *Varṇasūtras*[16] (Tib. *yi-ge'i mdo* means 'sūtras on phonemes') the *dhātusūtras*[17] (Tib. *dbyiṅs-kyi-mdo* 'lexicon of verbal roots') and the *uṇādisūtras*[18] (Tib. uṇ-(la)-sogs-kyi-mdo). Of the commentaries on the *sūtra*-text both Bu. and Ko. mention the Vṛtti by Dharmadāsa [in six thousand verses (Bu)] and sub-commentaries by Ratnamati [in twelve thousand verses (Bu)] and Pūrṇacandra [in thirty-six thousand verses (Bu)]

In recent discussion doubts have risen concerning Candragomin's authorship of the *Cāndra-vṛtti,*[19] these very references in Tibetan sources (Bu. and Ko.) figure prominently as text-external arguments in favour of assumption of a different author for the *Cāndravṛtti,* namely Dharmadāsa.[20] The relatively few text-internal indications pro and contra the identity of author of *sūtras* and *vṛtti* have so far not allowed for a definitic solution of the problem.[21] Sanskrit mss. of *Cāndra* commentaries by Ratnamati[22] and Pūrṇacandra[23] have been brought to light, but sufficient research has not yet been done on them possibly the commentaries of Ratnamati and Pūrṇacandra complement each other (Ranamati covering the section I.1 to VI-3, Pūrṇacandra commenting only on the final sub-chapters i.e. VI-4),[24] but it may not be ruled out that—Pūrṇacandra had composd a sub-commentary on Ratnamati's commentary, as Bu. and Ko. seem to suggest.[25] Besides, But-stona mentions an *Upasargavṛtti,*[26] a commentary on the verbal prepositions' and some works on nominal declension[27] verbal conjugation[28] that are supplementary texts in the *Cāndra* system of Sanskrit grammar.

Only Ko. mentions some names of Tibetan scholars who were active in the transmission of the *Cāndra* system of grammar into Tibet. He attributes the first translation of the basic text to the great translator *śon-ston-rdo-rje-rgyal-mtshan* (13th century A.D.).[29] The translation does not seem to have been preserved. As such: CH III / 10 is a revised version of his translation.

Further, Ko. names three Tibetan scholars who themselves have written commentaries on Cāṇdra grammar. They are *thugs-rje-dpal, zha-lu chos-skyoṅ-bzaṅ-po* and *Dharmākara. Thugs-rje-dpal* is the translator of two grammatical works, viz., the *byiṅs-kyi-tshogs* (Skt. *Dhātukāya*)[30] and the *tsandra-pa'i-uṇ-la-sogs-pa'i-'grel-pa-zhes-bya-ba* (Skt. *Cāndrasyo-ṇāder Vṛtti-nāma*).[31] The former is a work on the verbal roots of the Cāndra system and the later is a commentary on the *Uṇādi sūtra* of the same system. *Zha-lu chos-skyoṅ-bzaṅ-po* is the famous translator and grammarian from *zha-lu* during early 15th century A.D. The Sanskrit Version of the name is Dharmapālabhadra and he has contributed four translations on Sanskrit grammar viz., Ch III/12, CH III /13, CH VI/1 and CH VI/2. Out of these four works the first two works are affiliated to the *Cāndra* system and the last two are belong to a new system i.e *Manjuśrīvyākaraṇa.* The third scholar can be identified as the famous Tibetan grammarian and translator *Si-tu pan-chen, (Mahāpaṇḍita) chos-kyi-'byuṅ-gnas* (skt. Dharmākara) alias *gtsug-lag chos-kyi-snaṅ-ba*[32] (beginning of 18th century A.D.), who is mainly known as a major authority on Tibetan grammar[33] and as composer of the *dkar-chag* (Catalogue) of the *sde-dge-bkan-'gyur,*[34] but who was also expert in Sanskrit Linguistics, as exemplified by his masterly translation of the *Amarakośa* (Tib. chi-med-mdsod) lexicon.[35] In fact this famous scholar had devoted the later forty years of his life for Sanskrit studies. He endavoured to revise the extant canonical translations of Sanskrit treatises on grammar, Lexicograpy and *poetics,* Probably the commentary intended by Ko. is the treatise: *legs-par-sbyar-ba'i-sgra'i-bstan-bcos-tsaṇdra-pa'i-rnam-bśad-brda-sprod-gzhuṅ-lugs-rgya-mtshor-'jug-ciṅ-legs-bśad-rin-chen-'dren-pa'i'-gru-gziṅs,* which is a commentary on Cāndravyākaraṇa in three volumes.[36] However, no copies have come to light so far of the former two commentaries by *thugs-rje-dpal* and *zha-lu chos-skyoṅ-zbaṅ-po*. Now we want to discuss the 19 works, which belong to Cāndra school of Sanskrit grammar in detail.

CH III/1:

Tittle luṅ-du-ston-pa-tsandra-pa'i-mdo
"Sūtras of Cāndra grammar"
[Pek. 5767, Nā, 3759]
Skt. *Cāndra-vyākaraṇa-sūtras*
Author: Candragomin
Translator/s: Jetakarṇa and *Ñi-ma-rgyal-mtshan*
Place: thar-pa-gliṅ
Date: 13th/14th Century A.D.

The basic text of Cāndra's grammar has short prescriptive sūtras (Tib. *mdo*) concerning morphology, morphophonemics and semantics of classical Sanskrit. This basic text has been edited along with its commentaries. The present translation of this grammar is divided into six chapters *(adhyāyas)* Tib. *le'u)* and each chapter, further, is divided into four sub-chapters (*pādas;* Tib. *rkaṅ-pa*). The third chapter is incorporated with only seventeen sūtras of the twelveth sub-chapter and thus it is incomplete.

A close study of this grammar enable us to suggest that the whole text is divided into two parts on the ground of morphology and morphophonimics. The first four chapters deal with the former and the later is dealt in the next two chapters.

The first three sub-chapters are incorporated with primary suffixes (mainly nominal), and the fourth sub-chapter deals with conjugations. Declension, nominal composition the formation of feminine nominal stems are incorporated in the next three sub-chapters. Next nine sub-chapters (i.e. from 9th sub-chapter to 16th sub-chapter) deal with secondary nominal suffixes. The sūtras on morphophonemics are the subject of the rest sub-chapters, i.e. from 17th to 24th sub-chapters).

Besides the present translation of the Cāndra grammar, we have also a second translation (CH III/10). The subject matter of that work is the same as in the present translation; but the translator of the text was different (Please refer CH III /10).

The colophon of this work suggests that the translation of the *Cāndra sūtras* were done having received personal instructions from the great Brāhmin Paṇḍit Jetakarṇa (13th Century A.D.) from Nepal.[37] The same source, further, mentions that Jetakarṇa was a crown-jewel among the gammarians.[38] The whole work was translated into Tibetan at *thar-pa-gliṅ* monastery by monk *ñi-ma-rgyal-mtshan* (13th-14th century A.D.)[39]

The *thar-pa-gliṅ* monastery was located some miles south-west of *zha-lu* in gtsaṅ province. This *tha-pa-gliṅ* was the residence of *thar-pa-lo-tsā-ba* where *ñi-ma-rgyal-mtshan* and *bu-ston rin-chen-grup* received most of their tutelage in Sanskrit grammar from *thar-pa-lo-tsā-ba* in this monastery.[40]

The exact date of the translation of the work is not mentioned either in the text or in any other contemporaries, but on the basis of the age of the translator, we may guess that the work was translated during the last half of the 13th or first quarter of 14th century A.D.[41]

Jetakarṇa is said to have studied with the translator *ñi-ma-rgyal-mtshan* in *kra-kha* (or: skra-kha) in the region of Kāthmāṇḍu (Tib. *yam-bu*). This *ñi-ma-rgyal-mtshan* can be identified as the prolific translator *thar-pa-lo-tsa-ba ñi-ma-gryal-mtshan*, a student of šes-rab-seṅ-ge (1251-1315) [cf; *deb-ther-sṅon-po* trl. Roerich (1949-53) entitled the Blue Annals: 792]. It is also known to us that our translator was the teacher of *bu-ston rin-chen-grub* (1290-1364 A.D.). He had instructed him linguistics for several years particularly the *Cāndra* and *Kātantra* systems of Sanskrit grammar [Ibid, 102, 793, 800]. This is known from the Blue Annals that the translator was the head of the *snar-thaṅ* monastery about eight years i.e. from 1305-1312 A.D. [Ibid: 282-83].

CH III/2:

Title *ñe-bar-bsgyur-ba-ñi-śu-pa'i-'grel-pa*
"Commentary on the twenty verbal prepositions"
/ Pek. 5768, Nā, 3760, De. 4270 /
Skt: Vimśatyupasargavṛtti
Author: Candragomin
Translator/s : Jetakarṇa and *ñi-ma-rgyal-mtshan*
Place: *thar-pa-gliṅ*
Date: 13th century A.D.

This is an explanatory work on twenty Sanskrit verbal prepositions (or prepositional prefixes) which are called in Sanskrit *Upasargas*. This treatise deals with the *Upasargas* one after the other, enumerating their various denotations (in Tibetan) and giving examples (in Sanskrit and Tibetan) of each denotation. These twenty upasargas are : *pra* (Tib. rab-tu).*para* (mchog-tu) *apa* (lhag-par, *sam* (yaṅ-dag-par), and (rjes-su), *ava* (phul-du), *nir* (bral-ba), *dur* (ṅan-pa), *vi* (rnam-par), ā (ṅ) legs-par) *ni* (ñe-par), *adhi* (śin-tu), *api* (slar), *ati* (dag-par) *su* (bde-par), *ut* (mtho-bar), *abhi* (mṅon-par), *prati* (so-sor), *pari* (yoṅs-su) and *upa* (ṅes-bar).

In the Cāndra vyākaraṇavṛtti (Cā I, 1, 109) we have also a list of the twenty *upasargas* termed *prādi* and the ordering of this list differs slightly from the present list mentioned above.[42] In the former treatise there is *ni* immediately after *api*.[43] There is also a separate work on the *upasargas* entitled the *Upasarga-lakṣaṇa bhāṣya* (Cf; CH VII /5), where we have a different order of the *upasargas*. Again, it is to mark that there are a lot of differences in the Manuscripts of the treatise incorporated in Peking and Co-ne editions of the bstan-'gyur. As per the example at the beginning we have the Sanskrit forms of the *upasargas* in the Peking edition and the Tibetan translations of these forms are found in the Co-ne edition. In the colophon also there is an additional verse in the Co-ne edition. This work was also translated by *ñi-ma-rgyal-mtshan* with the help from Jetakarṇa.[44]

Refer CH III /1 for the personal life of the translators and for the geographical location of the place of translation.

CH III/3: *yi-ge'i-mdo*

"Sūtras on phonemes" [Pek. 5769, Nā, 3761, De-4271]

Skt: *Varṇa-sūtra*

Author: Candragomin

Translator/s: *ñi-ma-rgyal-mtshan*

Place: *gdud-phubs*

Dat: 14th century A.D.

This is a short work with rules on the phonology of classical Sanskrit and it belongs to the Cāndra system of Sanskrit grammar. The Tibetan translation of this work contains only fortytwo sūtras in total. The introductory work of this text, which is missing in the Sanskrit mss., recurs in a slightly different translation in the treatise entitled: *Varṇasūtravṛtti* which is a commentary of this work (cf: CH III/4 below). It has been mentioned earlier that this work was composed by Candragomin as a suppliment to his sūtra text.

The colophon of the text suggests that monk *ñi-ma-rgyal-mtshan* had translated the text into Tibetan and the translator was not well versed in Sanskrit grammar. The same source further suggests that the whole work was translated at a place named *gdud-phubs*, the godly residence of the teacher of the translator. Again, the colophon narrates that his teacher was endowed with the virtuous elements typical for *Boddisattva*.[45] The name of his teacher was *śes-rab-seṅ-ge* (1251-1315 A.D.).46

It is interesting to mark that the translator had completed his works i.e. CH III / 1, 2 and 4 with the help of Nepali scholar Jetakarṇa but he had translated the present work alone (Please refer CH III /1 for his personal life).

It is not possible to identify the toponym of the place *gdug-phubs,* the godly residence of the teacher of the translator. On the basis of the colophon of CH III /4 we may assume that it was situated in the region of *guṅ-thaṅ* i.e. *guṅ-thaṅ-gi-sa-cha-slob-dpon-lhai-sku-mkhar-gdud-phubs*. *guṅ-thaṅ* is a name of a District in south-west of *gtsaṅ* province; but there is no well known place like *gdud-phubs* to be found in the District nowadays. Thus, our assumption is not so sound in identifying the actual location of the place of the translation.

CH III/4:

Title: *yī-ge'i mdo-'i-'grel-pa.*
"Commentary on the sūtras on phonemes".
Skt: Varṇasūtra-vṛtti [Pek. 5770, Nā-3762, De 4292]
Author: Chos-skyoṅ (Dharmapāla)
Translator/s: Jetakarṇa and *ñi-ma-rgyal-mtshan*
Place: *gdud-phubs.*
Date: 13th/14th century A.D.

This is a metrical commentary on the work *yī-ge'i-mdo* (III/3) with 119 verss.[46] Since it is a commentary on the Cāndra phonological statements it evidently belongs to the Cāndra system of grammar. The commentary is ascribed to *chos-skyoṅ* means projector of 'Dharma" possibly to be reconstructed as Dharmapāla.[47] It is also interesting to note that a later Tibetan translation (1516 first translation and revision in 1531 A.D.) of the same commentary on the *yī-géi-mdo* has also been included as CH III/19. However, there is no mention of an author like *chos-skyoṅ*, in fact in the translator's colophon it is explicitly attributed to Candragomin.[48]

According to the colophon the translator *ñi-ma-gryal-mtshan,* after having personal instruction from the great grammarian Jetakarṇa in the district *kra-kha* belonging to the region of the city *yam-bu* in Nepal, had translated the basic work (CH III/3) at *gdud-phubs*, the godly residence of his teacher in the region of *guṅ-thaṅ* and after that only the same translator had translated the present—text at noble *thar-pa-gliṅ;* a great monastic academy which is the residence of the greatest of the great scholars.[49] The same colophon suggest that the work mentioned above i.e. CH III/3 was translated at *gdud-phubs* and the present work was translated at *thar-pa-glin* monastery.[50] Though no date of translation is mentioned, still we may accept the date of the translator as the date of translation i.e. last half of 13th or 1st quarter of 14th century A.D.

CH III/5:

Title: *spyir-btaṅ-ba-yaṅ-dag-par-bsdus-pa-zhes-bya-ba.*
"Synopsis of the *adhikāra* sūtras"
[Pek: 5771, Nā-3763, De. 4273]
Skt. *Adhikāra-samgraha-nāma*
Author: Not mentioned.
Translator/s: *blo-gros-brtan-pa*
Place: *ye-raṅ*
Date: 13th/14th century A.D.

This is the Tibetan translation of the work entitled: *Adhikāra-samgraha-nāma* with six chapters (and four sub-chapters in each chapter). An *adhikāra sūtra* does not itself prescribe a grammatical operation, but its terms should be supplied in all the rules in the section it heads or governs. Pāṇini mentions the *adhikāra sūtras* as one of his techniques to achieve maximum economy of words in the *Aṣṭādhyāyī*. The work under discussion is a treatise on the *adhikāra sūtras* of the *Cāndra* system of Sanskrit grammar. The *sūtras* have been taken and enumerated one by one in the work. However, the original Ms. in Sanskrit, from which the Tibetan translation was done, is not available now. And the Tibetan version of the Ms. does not blar the name of the author of the work. Thus, it is not possible for us to infer the name of the author. However, some scholars opine that Candragomin himself was the author of this treatise, but here we do not agree with this view, yet we may not reach in conclusive to remark that who is the author of the work due to the lack of evidences.

In the colophon of the Tibetan translation of this work it has been mentioned that the monk *dpal-ldan glo-gros-brtan-pa* has perfectly translated the text in the city of ye-raṅ,51 which was a chief city of Nepal during the mediaeval period. Nothing more is known about the city from the colophon.

Our translator was a student of *śon-blo-gros-brtan-pa* (second half of 13th century,) *śes-rab-seṅ-ge* (1251 to 1315 A.D.) and translator *mchog-ldan,* who taught him Sanskrit grammar. Acquiring perfect knowledge of Sanskrit grammar he became one of the main exponents of Sanskrit Linguistics in Tibet. He had visited several times to Nepal and in fact he made two of his translations of grammatical treatises there (in Nepal) i.e. CH III/

5 and CH III/7. The former was translated at *ye-raṅ* and the later was translated at *rol-pa'i-groṅ-khyre* (Skt. *Lilanagara*).

Out of forty-seven grammatical works, he alone had translated eight of them into Tibetan viz; CH III/5, CH III/7, CH II/8, CH III/10, CH IV/3, CH IV/6, CH IV/7 and CH V/1.

CH III/6

Title: *rnam-dbye'i-tshig-le'ur-byas-pa*
'Verses on the case endings'
[Pek. 5772, Nā-3764, De-4274]
Skt.: Vibhakti-kārikā
Author: *phrog-byed-bzaṅ-po* /
seṅ-ge-bzaṅ-po (Simhabhadra. Haribhadra).
Translator/s : *sa-dbaṅ-bzaṅ-po* and *blo-gros-brtan-pa*
Place: In a chief city of Nepal
Date: Second half of 13th century A.D.

This is a treatise on declensions (Vibhakti) belonging to the Cāndra system of Sanskrit grammar. There are four sections in this work and the first chapter (adhyāya) bears a study on the masculines.[52] The second chapter is concerned with the sūtras relating to feminine[53] and the neuter nouns are dealt with in the third chapter.[54] The fourth and last chapter deals with so-called pronominal declension which applies to pronouns, certain adjectives and numerals.[55] In this work, the main points of the nominal declension are expounded by suitable examples[56]—preceded by often brief references to the *Cādra sūtras* that are applied—exemplary of the idiosyncracies of declension typical for the various types of stems. However, it is a great loss that the original Sanskrit work of this Ms. is not available either in printed form or in natural form.

In the introductory verse the author is referred to as 'the monk' *(dge-sloṅ) phrog-byed-bzaṅ-po*.[57] In the title caption in the Peking edition he is called Simhabhadra,[58] all consulted catalogues attribute the text to the 'master' (*slob-dpon) seṅ-ge-bzaṇ-po*. The famous scholar Liebich (1895: 19)prefers the word Iśvarabhadra as the Sanskrit reconstruction of the Tibetan name. However, as Tibetan word *phrog-byed* 'the robber' (generally equivalent to skt. *Hari*) can also denote 'lion'[59] (Skt. *Simha*,

Tibetan *seṅ-ge*), it seems more plausible that Simhabhadra (or Haribhadra) was the actual name of the author.

The colophon suggests that the work was completed in a city of Nepal which was situated in the lowermost part of Nepal *[bal-po'i-mthil]*. By the personal instruction from Nepalese scholar *dpal sa-dbaṅ-bzaṅ-po,* the Tibetan translator-monk *śoṅ-blo-gros-brtan-pa* has translated the work. Though the translator has not mentioned the place of translation, still we think the work perhaps was translated at *ye-raṅ*,[60] which may be identified as Patan (Refer CH III/7).

As it has been mentioned earlier that the translator of this work was the teacher of *blo-gros-brtas-pa.* The translator was the younger brother and disciple of *śoṅ-ston-rdo-rje-rgyal-mtshan* (13th century A.D.). He has contributed nine translation works to the *bstan-'gyur* seven in the *tantra* section and the rest two are Sanskrit linguistic treatises, viz., the CH III/6 and the Indian standard work on poetics, Daṇḍin's *Kāvyādarśa.* However, the translation of the *Kāvyādarśa* was done by his elder brother and he revised the work. In the Blue Annals, G.N. Roerich identifies *śoṅ blo-gros-brtan-pa* and *dpaṅ blo-gros brtan-pa* as one and same person; but we have ample indications that they were two different persons. Thus, we do not agree with Roerich's view.

CH III/7:

Title: *tiṅ'i-mtha'*
"(Forms) ending in ti(ṅ)"
[Pek. 5773, Nā. 3765, De-4275]
Skt. *Tinaṅta*
Author: *Dpal [Lakṣikara or Lakṣmiśrī]*
Translator/s: *dpal-ldan blo-gros-brtan-pa.*
Place: *rol-pa'i-groṅ-khyer* (in *bal-po'i-yul*). [Nepal]
Date: 13th/14th Century A.D.

This is a work on verbal conjugations and belongs to the Cāndra system of Sanskrit grammar. It is divided into ten sections and twenty sub-sections, consisting mainly of the paradigms of the ten tenses and moods,[62] each divided into the active and medial forms, of one root √pac 'to cook'. each paradigm is preceded by a brief description of the derivation procedure, quoting and paraphrasing *sūtra*s from Cāndra's grammar.

As the name of the author we have mere the designation Dpal (skt. 'Śrī').[63] This creates more problem to identify the author. However, Cordier, an Europian scholar identifies the author as Paṇḍita Lakṣmikara or Lakṣmiśrī from Nepal.[64] But he has not given any arguments in support of his identification.

It is known from the colophon that the Tibetan translator-monk *dpaṅ blo-gros-brtan-pa* has translated the text, revised the translation and had given a definite from to the work at *rol-pa'i-groṅ-khyer* [=Lalitapur] in the country of Nepal.[65] It is known from the "History of Nepal" that when Buddhism entered in Nepal, the "Buddhmārgis" and the "Śaivamārgis" became divided into two parties. After this occurrence the cities of Devapatan, kantipur, Lalitpur and Bhaktapur were built and peopled.[66] Again the history identifies the four town as Devapatan, Kathmandu, Patan and Bhatgaon.[67] Thus, the translation of the work was done at modern Patan of Nepal, which is situated in the Lower part of Nepal. Now, we may safely suggest that CH III/5 and CH III/6 were translated in the same place where CH III/7 was done.

Refer CH III/5 for the personal history of the translator.

CH III/8:

Title: *'brel-pa-mdor-bstan-pa*
"Brief expose of (syntactic) relations"
[Pek. 5774, Nā 3766, De. 4276]
Skt: Sambandhoddeśa
Author: Caṅgadāsa? [*Kā-yastha-tsākādāsa*]
Translator/s : *dpal-ldan blo-gros-brtan-pa*
Place: Not mentioned
Date: 13th/14th Century A.D.

This metrical work on syntactic relations belongs to the *Cāndra* system of Sanskrit grammar. It is divided into six sections [skt. *uddeśa*, Tib. *(mdor)-bstan-pa)*] dealing with syntactic relations in general,[68] syntactic relations in connection with verbal forms,[69] with primary nominal derivatives,[70] with nominal cass,[71] with nominal composition72 and with secondary nominal derivates73 respectively. There are sixty-one verses in this work. Thus it is a work in *Kārikā* (verse) form.

The original Sanskrit work which is still now in ms. form is called as Caṅgavṛtti / Caṅgasūtra / Vaiyākaraṇajīvatu / sambandhoddeśa.[74] The word *smabandha* can have various technical denotations in grammatical context. In the present context it cannot but be taken to denote 'syntactic relations'. In the Pāṇinian system it can denote 'connection in general.[75] [P. III-4-1]. Moreover, Bhartṛhari, a famous grammarian and Philosopher of 5th century A.D. devoted the third section of the third *kāṇḍa* of his work, entitled *sambandha samuddes'a,* to *sambandha* in the sense of *śabdārthasambandha* 'relation between word and its sense' which relation can be of various types.[76]

Though the title of the present work is similar to the *Sambandhasamuddeśa* of Bhartṛhari still these two are not identical at all. The present work deals with syntax not in an abstract way, but relates the semantic and syntactic phenomena frequently with the morphology involved, explicitly stating and enumerating suffixes and other morphological elements. The work of Bhartṛhari is, however, of a much abstract and of theoretical nature. It deals with linguistic—philosophical speculation, with relatively little attention for the specific morphological aspects.

It is known from the colophon that the present work was translated by *dpal-ldan blo-gros-brtan-pa.* Again, it is known from the same source that *śoṅ rdo-rje-rgydl-mtshan* had collected funds from various friends for the translation and brought the present form of this work.[77]

Refer CH III/5 for the personal life of the translator.

CH III/9:

Title: dbyiṅs-kyi-tshogs
"Corpus of verbal roots"
[Pek. 5893, Nā. 3885, De. 4429[.
Skt.: Dhātukāya
Author: Not mentioned
Translator/s: *(bu-ston) rin-chen-grub.*
Place: Not mentioned
Date: 14th century A.D. (1st half).

This is a catalogue of roots belonging to *Cāndra* system of grammar. Traditionally the catalogue of roots are called *dhātupāṭha.* A deep study on this subject enable us to remark that the Pāṇinian *dhātupāṭha*, the oldest known *dhātupāṭha,* is different from the *dhātupāṭha* of *Cāndra* system's and the present text is a version of the later.

Generally the roots are grouped into ten major classes (gaṇas),[78] corresponding to the ten different formations of the present indicative and the related tenses and moods. In the Cāndra system the ordering of roots differs considerably from that in the Pāṇinian dhātupāṭha.[79] The roots are invariably presented in three groups in this system viz., the active, medial and bimodal verbs respectively. In the present text we also find this ordering of roots as we find in the Cāndra system.

Another remarkable difference between the Pāṇinian and Cāndra *dhātupāṭha* is the fact that the later, with a few exceptions, gives only one sense per root,[80] while the former regularly quotes more than one sense for a single root.[81] Besides these two systems differ in number of roots. In the list of roots of the Pāṇinian system we find around 1950 roots,[82] where as the Cāndra's list contains considerably fewer roots, especially in the first and tenth roots class *(gaṇa).* The present version has 1618 roots.[83] This work was translated by Bu-ston.[84]

Bu-ston rin-chen-grub (1290-1364 A.D.) has contributed three translations to Sanskrit grammatical literature in Tibetan. These three works are: CH III/9 and CH IV/5 and-8. According to his biography which has been prepared by his student *sgra-tshad-pa rin-chen-rnam-rgyal* (1318-1388 A.D.), during 1312 to 1320 A.D., our translator intensively studied Sanskrit grammar, lexicography and various Indian systems of writing under *thar-pa-lo-tsā-ba ña-ma-rgyal-mtshan.*[85]

His translation CH IV/5 (of Durgasimha's commentary on Kātantra of Kalāpa), which has not been preserved in the xylographic editions of the *bstan-'gyur,* must have been made prior to 1335 A.D. (composition of the *dkar-chag*). Note that the biography states that around 1344 he translated the 'remainder' of Durgasimha's Kātantra commentary.

His other translations on Sanskrit grammar i.e. CH III/9 and CH IV/8, both *dhātupāṭhas* i.e. catalogues of verbal roots, are also included in the 1335 *dkar-chag.* The biography possibly refers to later revision work on one or either of them in 1362 A.D.[86]

CH III/10:

Title: *luṅ-(du-) ston-pa-tsāndra-pa'i-mdo*
"Cāndra grammatical rules"
[De. 4269, Co. RE 1]
Skt: Cāndra-vyākaraṇa-sūtra
Author: Candragomin
Translator/s:
Original: *śoṅ-ston rdo-rje-rgyal-mtshan*
revisor: *dpal-ldan blo-gros-brtan-pa.*
Place: Not mentioned
Date: 13th/14th century A.D.

This is the basic text of the *Cāndra* system of Sanskrit grammar and is quite same as CH III/1. This translation is different from CH III/1. CH III/1, occurring in the *Peking* (Pek.) and *snar-thaṅ* (Nā) editions of the *bstan-'gyur,* is a translation done by *thar-pa-lo-tsā-ba ñi-ma-rgyal-mtsha,* in cooperation with Jetakarṇa. However, CH III/10 occurs in the *Co-ne* and *sde-dge* editions only. It is a different and distinctly more accurate translation of the same work, originally made by *śoṅ-ston rdo-rje-rgyal-mtshan* and revised by *blo-gros-brtan-pa.* Thus, the colophon of the text states that *śoṅ-ston rdo-rj-rgyal-mtshan,* the master of the translators had translated the text (for the first time) and that was revised by the above said scholar, viz., *skad-gñis-smra-ba'i-dbaṅ-po-śoṅ-ston-rdo-rje-rgyal-mtshan-gyis-legs-par-bsgyur-ba-las / slar-yaṅ-dpal-ldan-blo-gros-brtan-pas-bsgyur-ciṅ-zhus-te-gtan-la-phab-pa'o /*
[Co. 31 r 7].

śoṅ-ston rdo rje-rgyal-mtshan was a prominent Tibetan translator in the second half of the 13th Century A.D. and first quarter of 14th century A.D. He was a student of *stag-sde-ba-seṅ-ge-rgyal-mtshan* (1212-1294). Tibetan historiography often describes him as the founder or one of the founders of Sanskrit linguistic studies in Tibet, encompassing not only grammar, but also lexicography, prosody and rhetorics.[87]

CH III/11:

Title: *dbyiṅs-kyi-tshogs*
"Corpus of verbal roots" [De. 4277, Co. RE 9]
Skt.: *Dhātu-kāya.*

Author: [Purṇacandra?]
Translator/s: *thugs-rje-dpal-bzaṅ-po.*
Place: *e-chos-byuṅ-ba.*
Date: 14th/15th Century A.D.

This is a catalogue of verbal roots of Cāndra system of grammar (Cf; CH III/9 and 14 and CH IV/8). Here the name of the author has not been stated in any way. Since it belongs to Cāndra system, we may infer that Candragomin was its author. In the colophon it has been mentioned that: *tsandra-pa'i'byiṅs-kyi-mdo-rdzogs-so:*[88] means—"The *dhātu sūtras* of the Cāndra system have been completed. Again the colophon remarks that the present text is an essence of *Candra'sdhātupāṭha* written by master Purṇacandra and has been translated in the famous monastery *e-chos-byuṅ-ba.*[89] It was translated by *thugs-rje-dpal (bzaṅ-po)* and the translation work was completed on the auspicious moment of the twenty-fourth day of the month of *tha-skar* of the water male-dragon year called *dga-ba,* under the constellation of *rgyal* (puṣya), the eighth on, on the day of Jupiter (Thursday). This may be identified as A.D. 1352 Or A.D. 1412. However, the translation was done either in the last half of 14th century A.D. or in the first half of 15th century A.D.

thugs-rje-dpal-bzaṅ-po perhaps the same person as the *thugs-rje-dpal* who was on of the compilers of a *bka'-'gyur* catalogue issued in *rgyal-rtse* by the king *rab-brtan-kun-bzaṅ-phags.* (last half of 14th to 1st half of 15th Century A.D.) Besides, he had translated two other texts: one on *tantra* and the other on *sūtra* and these two are included in the *bstan-'gyur* [Peking Edition]. However, our work is included only in the *sde-dge* and *Co-ne* editions of the *bstan-'gyur.*

E-chos-byuṅ-ba is the location where five grammatical texts viz., CH III/11, CH III/15, CH III/16, CH IV/11 and CH/12 were translated into Tibetan. Besides, it is also mentioned in an intermediate colophon of a text i.e. CH IV/6. It is variously designated as: *dpal-e-chos-'byuṅ-ba'i-gtsug-lag-khaṅ-chen-po* in CH III/11 (Co. 85 v 4), *dpal-e'i-gtsug-lag-khaṅ* in CH IV/12 (Pek. 352 v 8) *dpal-e'i-chos-gra* in CH IV/11 (Pek. 304 r4) and *dpal-e'i-chos-grwa-chen-po* in CH III/15 and 16 (Pek. 369 v6 and 419 v4).

The identification of this monastic institution has some problems. However, on the basis of our study we prefer to identify this with the *bo-doṅ-e* monastery in *gtsaṅ* province.

CH III/12:

Title: *lbrel-ba-grub-pa-zhes-bya-ba'i-rab-tu-byed-pa.*
"The technical derivational procedure".
[De. 4278, Co. RE 10].
Skt: Sambandha-siddhi-abhidhāna-prakriyā.
Author: *ñi-mái-sñiṅ-po*
Translator/s: (zha-lu) dharmapālabhadra.
Place: *(pho-braṅ) se'u-gdar-rtse.*
Date: 15th Century A.D.

This is the translation of a commentary of a text dealing with syntax and morphology. Its main characteristic is that it follows the system of Pāṇini and Cāndra. The basic text, on which the commentary was prepared, was a text in verse form. It is known from *bstan-'gyur* that the present work is similar to two other works (refer CH I/1 and CH VII/6). The text is incorporated with case, nominal composition, *taddhita* secondary derivations, verbal morphology and finally primary nominal derivations. Thus we may divide the whole text into five major chapters. it is to mark that before commenting on the text, the writer writs the whole basic text at the beginning of this text.

Though the work is similar to CH II/1, still it is to mark that while in CH II/1 we find the Tibetan translation of the examples, in this treatise we have a large number of the examples in original Sanskrit form. The text (CH VII/6), is not so elaborate like the present one. The present translation is more similar to CH VII/6 than CH II/1.

Though the present work is the essence from Cāndra and Pāṇini's system still the colophon suggests that it belongs to the Cāndra school.[90] In the colophon, the translator gives a nice introduction to the work including the author's name, place of translation and subject matter of the text.[91] The author i.e. *ñi-mái-sñiṅ-po* (colophon) is also credited with another work (refer CH VII/6).

According to colophon, the translator of the work is Dharmapālabhadra. He had completed the task on the request of Dharma-kīrtijñānaśrībhadra, the fourth holder of the crown which is the 'Red Hat' *(Zhwa-dmar)*, the precious reincarnation who was the lord of *dharma* 'justice'.[92] According to the same source the author was from *gos* family and had studied the grammatical literature properly before translating the text and during his duration he received *dge-tshul* ordination at twenty one in 1462 A.D.[93] and that of *dge-sloṅ* at twentysix in 1467 A.D.[94] He studied Sanskrit grammar from 1465 onwards and after his *dge-sloṅ* ordination he continued his grammatical studies under *stag-tshaṅ-lo-tsā-bsa-śes-rab-rin-chen* on certain aspects of Kātantra, and under *dpal-ldiṅs-lo-tsā-ba grags-pa-blo-gros* the Cāndra system. From 1465 to 1501, he worked in *dpal-'khor-chos-sde* on numerous revisions of translations within the *bká-gyur*. In his later age he resided in *ri-phug* hermitage of *zha-lu* monastery and in *rste-gdoṅ*, where he taught various linguistic science.[95]

Eleven translation works have been contributed by him to the Peking edition of the bstan-'gyur; three in *tantra* section and eight in sūtra section. It is interesting that in this edition only two grammatical translations are attributed to his name. (Cf. CH VI/1-2) and in the Co-ne edition and in the *sde-dge* edition, two more translations on Sanskrit grammar are included and the present work is one of them.

The colophon of this work, further, suggests that all kinds of help were given for this translation in the monastic academy of palace *se'u-gdar-rtse*, the residence of the two classes (i.e. laical and clerical), of *dpal ṅag-gi-dbaṅ-phyug-grags-pa-phyogs-thams-cad-las-rnam-par-rgyal-ba.* Again, form the same source it is known that after comparison with an old Indian manuscript, corrections in the translation and minor revisions were established [cf; Co. 114 v3-4].

CH III/13:

Title: *u-ṇā-la-sogs-pāi-grel-pa*
"Commentary on the Uṇādisūtras"
(De. 4279, Co. RE 11)
Skt. Uṇādisūtravṛtti.
Author: Candragomin

Translator/s: *(zha-lu) rin-chen-chos-skyoṅ-bzaṅ-po.*
Place: *grwa-phyis-gzhis-pa-lhun-grub-gliṅ.*
Date: 15th century A.D. (Last quarter)

This is a commentary on the *Uṇādisūtras* of the Cāndra system of Sanskrit grammar. The *Uṇādisūtras* follow that view that nouns are derived from the verbal roots. The Uṇādi suffixes and the nominal bases drived with them are considered more or less anamalous, so that they are not dealt with in the mainbody of the sūtra text of the various grammatical systems, but are generally grouped in a separate corpus of *sūtras.* The present work which is attributed to Candragomin, has survived in two incomplete Sanskrit manuscripts (only some folios from the beginning and the commentary on II-103 up III-7 are missing). However, the Sanskrit text has not been edited and only the examples are given in the edition of the Cāndra Uṇādi sūtras. Th attribution of the present commentary to Candragomin can not be deemed certain as his authorship of the text commented upon is quite uncertain as well. Beside the present work a Tibetan translation of the Cāndra *Uṇādi sūtra* text (cf; CH. III/15) and another translation of the commentary (CH III/16) have also even included in *bstan-'gyur.*

According to the colophon befor this work, two more translations of this treatise were made by two scholars and those two were not so perfect and were incomplete. This work was done by *rin-chen-chos-skyoṅ-dpal-bzaṅ-po* from zha-lu to full fill the mentioned gap. This is also known from the colophon that the work was done on the basis of an Indian manuscript (in Sanskrit), written by Candragomin.

Regarding the date of translation of the work the colophon suggests that it has been expounded in *grwa-phyis-gzhis-pa-lhun-grub-gliṅ*, on the fifteen day of the white (part) of the month *chu-stod* (i.e. the sixth month) of the year called *gal-syed,* seven cycles of sixty (years) and forty-four single (years) after (the beginning of) the *rab-byuṅ* the year of the death of *me-mkha-rgya-mtsho* (A.D. 1491?).[97]

The translator had completed this work with the royal assistance of *kun-dga-bsod-nams-rin-chen,* the noble lord of men. He had given very assistance to complete the treatise.[98]

Refer CH III/12 for the personal life of the translator.

CH III/14: Title: *byiṅs-mdo*
"Sūtras on verbal roots"
[Pek 5887, Nā, 3879, De. 4424]
Skt. Dhātu-sūtra
Author: *gaṅ-ba'i-zla-ba'i zhabs* (Pūrṇacandrapāda).
Translator/s: *byaṅ-chub-rtse-mo*
Copyist: *grub-pa-mgon-bzaṅ-po*
Place: Not mentioned
Date: 14th Century A.D.

This is a work on the verbal roots and it belongs to the Cāndra system of Sanskrit grammar. Liebich opines that the present version is probably the finest form of the Cāndra *dhātupāṭha* in the Tibetan Canonical literature.[99] Dr. Bhattacharya has edited a portion of the work along with its restoration into Sanskrit.

Though, the Cāndra *dhātupāṭha* is considered to be the work of Candragomin, the founder of the Cāndra system of Sanskrit grammar, still the colophon of this work suggests that the present treatise is a product of Pūrṇacandra (pāda)[Tib.: *gaṅ-ba'i-zla-ba (zhabs)*].[100] Pūrṇacandra is known as the author of a commentary on the *dhātupāṭha* entitled *Dhātupārāyaṇa*, which is generally associated with Cāndra system. Again, the same author is also referred to in the colophon of *Dhātu-kāya*. There it has been mentioned that the work i.e. CH III/1 is based on the work Cāndra *dhātupāṭha* of Pūrṇacandra. Thus, our author was a master on verbal roots and had composed a version of the Cāndra *dhstupāṭha* and a commentary on it called Dhātupārāyaṇa. Now we may suggest that the present work is bassd on the later work of Pūrṇacandra. According to the N. Cat. Cat. (Vol. IX-290) the Dhatupārāyana is a work on the verbal roots of Cāndra system; composed in 10th century A.D. by Pūrṇacandra.[101]

See CH IV/6 for the personal history of the translator.

CH III/15
Title: *uṇ-la-sogs-pa'i-mdo*
"The Uṇ and others sūtras"
Skt.: *Uṇādisūtras*
Author: Candragomin

Translator/s: *nam-mkha'-bzaṅ-po.*
Place: *e'i-chos-grwa-chen-po*
Date: 14th century A.D.

This is a text on the *Uṇādi sūtras* of the *Cāndra* system of Sanskrit grammar and it is attributed to Candragomin the author of the Cāndra sūtra text. In the text, the suffix introduced in the first sūtra is -uṇ-, hence the designation of the text is *uṇādi* means uṇ and other suffixes'.

The Sanskrit basic text of the Cāndra *uṇādi sūtras* has been edited by Liebich in early twenties. The sūtras in the text are divided into four chapters *(pādas)*. Unlike the ordering in Pāṇini's Uṇādi sūtras, the order in which the suffixes are represented in the present treatise is determined by the final morpheme of the suffix. The first chapter deals with the suffixes ending in any vowel but (in this order: u, ū, ṛ, i, Ī, a, o and au), the second chapter with part of the suffixes ending in 'a' (general alphabetical order) from 'ka' to 'ya', the chapter three with the remainder of the suffixes ending in 'a' viz; from *ura* to *ha* and the zero-suffix termed *kvip*, as well as suffixes ending in consonant (again in general alphabetical order, from *-c* to *-s)*.

According to the colophon, the text has been translated by *nam-mkha-bzaṅ-po* at the famous monastery of *e'i-chos-grwa-chen-po.* Though the translator or any contemporary scholars have not mentioned the date of the translation, still we may opine that the work was completed in 14th century A.D. as the translator of the text was flourished during this time.

Refer CH IV/12 for the personal life of the translator and for geographical location of the place of translation refer CH III/11 above.

CH III/16

Title: *tshāndra-pa'i-uṇ-la-sogs-pa'i-grcl-pa (-zhes-bya-ba)*
"Commentary on Cāndra Uṇādi sūtras'
[Pek. 5891, Nā. 3883, De. 4428]
Skt: *Cāndrasya Uṇāder-vṛtti*
Author: Candragomin?
Translator/s: *thugs-rje-dpal-bzaṅ-po*
Place: *e'i-chos-grwa.*
Date: 14th/15th century A.D.

This is a commentary on the above mentioned (CH III/15) text of Candragomin with three chapters (pāda)./ The commentary is also attributed to the author of the text. In the present translation the author's name is not explicitly referred to. In fact, the colophon states that in the Indian manuscript the author's name is missing. The whole work has been translated by *thugs-rje-dpal-bzaṅ-pa.*

Refer CH III/11 for the life of the translator and CH IV/6 for the geographical location of the place of translation.

CH III/17

Title: *su-pa'i-mtha-rin-chen-byuṅ-gnas (-zhes-bya-ba).*
"The Jewel-mine of words ending in "sup".
[Pk.: 5894, Nā. 3886, De. 4430]
Skt.: *Subanta-ratnākara-nāma*
Author: Not mentioned
Translator/s: Not mentioned
Place: Not mentioned
Date: Not mentioned

"Sup" is a technical abbreviated term of the suffixes functioning as the case-endings, hence the word *supanta* "ending in a *sup*" refers to nouns or rather the bound syntactic forms of nouns. Thus, the present treatise is an incomplete work on nominal declension in classical Sanskrit. This belongs to the Cāndra system of grammar.

The structure of the work is similar to that of sl. nos. CH III/6, CH IV/7, and CH IV/10 (that follows Kalāpa grammar) and CH III/18 (that follows Cāndra system). This is an incomplete work and it is incorporated with only two sections *(pādas)* on masculine ending in vowels and masculine ending in consonants. The first section is also incomplete and it deals with the declension of masculine nouns ending in vowel with ten -sub-sections, final vowel a, ā, i, ī, u, ū, ṛ, ai, o and au.102 Th text breaks off in the middle of the second section, on the declension of masculine nouns ending consonants. The second section has five sub-sections on final 'c', 'j', 't', 'd' and'dh' and the text breaks off abruptly in the sixty sub-sections, on masculine nouns ending in '-n'.[103] This second section bears six sub-sections.

Ch III/18

Title: *luṅ-du-ston-pa-su-panta (-zhes-bya-ba).*
"Grammatical work with words ending in 'sup' "
[Pek. 5895, Nā, 3887, De. 4431]
Skt. *Vyākaraṇa-supanta-nāma*
Author: Not mentioned.
Translator/s: Not mentioned
Place: Not mentioned
Date: Not mentioned

Like the above work, this is also a treatise on nominal declensions and it follows the Cāndra system. The present work is similar in contents and structure to the preceding work CH III/17. It is a special feature of the present treatise that in the synoptic description of the derivational procedure that proceeds the paradigms the required Cāndra sūtras are often quoted in Sanskrit.

The work is incomplete. It has two complete sections and one incomplete section in total. The first section deals with the declension of masculine nouns ending in vowels. This opening section is incorporated with twelve sub-sections dealing with stems ending in a *(rudra)*, ā *(hāhā)*, i *(agni, sakhi, pati)*, u *(bhānu)*, ū *(pratibhū)*, ṛ *(pitṛ, praśastṛ)* ai *(rai)*, o *(go)*, au *(glau)*.[104] The second section deals with the declension of masculine nouns ending in consonants. The second section is divided into fortyfive sub-sections on systems ending in c *(jalamuc, kruñc)*, j *(bhubhuj, svārāj)* t *(marut)*, d *(kravyad)*, dh *(mṛgavyadh)*, n *(brahman, rājan, śvan, maghavan, pathin, pūsan, vṛtrahan* and *pathin)* ś (viś), ṣ (dviṣ), s *(uedhas, uśanas, pums)* h *(anaḍvaḥ, madhuliḥ mitraduḥ)* kṣ *(kāṣthatakṣ)*.[105] The third section dals with the declncion of neuter nouns (example: *manas*).[106]

CH III/19

Title: *luṅ-ston-pa-tsāndra-pa'i-yi-ge'i-mdo-'grel-pa.*
"Commentary on the sūtras o phonemes of the Cāndra system".
[Pek: 5902, Nā 3894, De. 4458]
Skt.: *Cāndra-vyākaraṇa-varṇa-sūtra-vṛtti*
Author: Candragomin

Translator/s: *ṅag-dbaṅ-rin-chen-bkra-śis-dpa-bzaṅ-po.*
Place: *gra-thaṅ-jam-dbyaṅś-dgyes-pa'i-gtsug'-lag-khaṅ.*
Date: 16th century [1516 first translation and 1531 revision]

This is a commentary on the *varṇa sūtras* belonging to the Cāndra system of grammar. Earlier, it has been mentioned that during the early phase a text and a commentary on the *varṇa sūtras* were translated into Tibetan (CH III/3 and CH III/4). It is known from the colophon of the present text that this type of work has been translated into Tibetan for the first time.[107] It may be suggested that the translator was not aware enough about the works those were translated into Tibetan from Sanskrit before or during his age. Thus, the translation of the work entitled: *varṇasūtravṛtti* of Dharmpāla (?) (CH III/4), which formed part of the earliest edition of *bstan-'gyur*, many have not known to the translator of present work viz., *skyogs-ston ṅag-dbaṅ-rin-chen-bkra-śis,* a personal pupil of the famous grammarian zha-lu Dharmapālabhadra and author of the well-known Lexicon *li-śi-'i-gur-khaṅ.*

It is also to mark that the author of the text referred to in the colophon of the work CH III/4 as *chos-skyoṅ,* i.e., Dharmapāla? and in the present text he is not mentioned at all, but here in the colophon we find Candragomin as the author of the original text.108

Our author was the translator of only one text on Sanskrit grammar (i.e. present text). According to the colophon of the work, he made his first version of translation of the instigation and under direct supervision of *zha-lu-chos-skyoṅ-bzaṅ-po* (15th to 16th century A.D.) in the year 1516,[109] he apparently was a personal disciple of zha-lu. From the same source it is also known to us that the second version of the translation was completed in the year 1531.[110] Thus, the translator had taken 10 years to revise the work and to give a complete and definite shape of the work. The author is primarily known as the author of a Tibetan Lexicographical work commonly entitled as *li-śi'i-gur-khaṅ.* This work was completed in the year 1536. Thus, the lexicon was composed during his last age. Though the exact date of his demise is not known to us, still we opine that he was died after 1536. Thus he flourished in between of second half of 15th century A.D. to first half of 16th century A.D.

While the first version was composed at *gra-thaṅ* monastery, the second version was completed at *jam-dbyaṅs-dgyes-pái-gtsug-lag-khaṅ*, the great monastery of the noble *Karma-pa* sect, situated in the outskirits of the districts of the region *ñaṅ-po*.

Notes and References

1. Cf; Coward, H.G. and Raja, K.K. (eds) The *Philosophy of the Grammarians; Encyclopedia* of Indian Philosophies, Delhi, 1990, p. 18.
2. Cf; Tatz, M; on the date of Candragomin, in H.C. Das, C. Das and S.S.R. Paul (Eds.); Buddhism and Jainism, pat 1, Cuttack, 1976, pp. 281-297.
3. Cf; Tatz, M; The Life of Candragomin in Tibetan Historical Tradition, *Tibet Journal* VII, 3, 1982, p. 3.
4. Refer; Obermiller, E; Hisory or Buddhism (chos ᶜbyuṅg) by Bu-ston, part IInd, Heidelberg, 1931-1932, p. 132.
5. Refer, Tatz, M; 1982, pp. 7-8.
6. Refer, Dash, N.K; 1990, pp. 54 and 57; Dwivedi, J.P; Buddhist Grammarians, Commentators and Tibetan Translators (in Hindi), Sarnath, 1987, pp. 13 to 17.
7. Refer; Dwivedi, J.P., 1987, pp. 23-33.
8. Refer; Keith, A.B; A History of Sanskrit literaturee, Oxford, 1928, p. 431.
9. Tazt, M; 1976, p. 287 and 1982, p. 11.
10. Vide; Chatterjee, K.C; (Ed) Cāndravyākaraṇa of Candragomin, pt. 1 (Chapters 1-3), Poona, 1953, p. 1.
11. Cf; Obermiller, E; 1931-1932, Part-IInd, pp. 132-33.
12. Cf; Scharfe, H; Grammatical Literature, A Hisotry of Indian Literature, Vol. V, Facs 2 (Ed. J. Gonda) Wiesbaden, 1977, p. 164, also refer Dwivedi, J.P. 1987, p. 65.
13. Cf; Bu-ston bstan-'gyur-dkar-chag, ed. Chandra, L; 1971, Vol. 26: 626 5-6, LA 113 V5-6.
14. Tazt, M; 1976, p. 291.
15. Cf; Obermiller, E; 1931-32, Part IInd, pp. 133, 168-69. and also Cf; Chandra, L; 1970, Vol. 1: 555. 1-2.
16. Cf; CH III/3 and also CH III/4 and CH III/19.
17. Cf; CH III/9, CH III/11, CH III/14 and also CH IV/8 CH III/11.
18. Cf; CH III/15 and also CH III/13, CH III/16.

19. Cf; Chatterjee, K.C.; 1953 (introduction) and Dash, P.C; A comparative study of the Pāṇinian and Cāndra Systems of Grammar (*Kṛdanta* portion), Delhi, 1986, pp. 17-21.
20. Cf; Tazt, M; 1976; p. 288.
21. Cf; Oberlies, T; Studie zum Cāndravyākarana Eine Kritische Barbeitung von Cāndra IV -4-52-148 and V.2, Stuttgart, 1989. pp. 2-4 and 8.
22. Cf; Sāṅkṛtyāyana, R; Second Search of Sanskrit Plam-leaf mss. in Tibet, J.B.O.R.S., Vol. XXIII, 1935, pp. 1-59 (p. 43 no. 294).
23. Cf; Ibid (p. 43 no. 296).
24. Cf; Oberlies, T; 1989. pp. 27-28.
25. Cf; *de-la-slob-dpon-rin-chen-blo-gros-zhes-pas-'grel-bśad-śo-lo-ka-lo-stoṅ-phrag-bcu-gñis-pa-mdzad / de-la-paṇḍita-zla-ba-gaṅ-ba-zhes-pas-'grel-bśad-kyi-bśad-pa-śo-lo-ka-lo-sum-khri-drug-stoṅ-pa-zhig-mdzad-do* / Ed. Chandra I; Vo. 24, 1965-71; 864. 6-7, 116v 6-7.
26. Cf; CH III/2 and CH VII/5.
27. Cf; CH III/6, CH III/17, and CH III/18.
28. Cf; CH III/7.
29. Cf; CH III/10.
30. Cf; CH III/11.
31. Cf; CH III/16.
32. His full ordination names were: (1) *Chos-kyi-'byuṅ-gnas-phrin-las-kun-khyab-ye-śes-dpal-bzaṅ-po* and *Karma-bstan-pa'i-ñin-byed-gtsug-lag-chos-kyi-snaṅ-ba*. Various other combinations of detachable parts of these names are used as well; Cf; Smith, E.G., introduction to Chandra, L (ed.); The Autobiography and Diaris of *si-tu paṇ-chen;* New Delhi, 1968, p. 9.
33. Cf; Miller, R.A.; The Si-tu Mahāpaṇḍita on Tibetan phonology in Dr. Hachiro Yuasa: A collection of papers commemortating his seventieth Anniversary, Tokyo, 1962, pp. 921-933.
34. Cf; Vostrikov, A.I.; Tibetan Historical literature, (trn. from Russian by H.C. Gupta) Calcutta, 1970, pp. 210-12.
35. For the full title please refer Ghosh, B.S. article Study of Sanskrit grammar in Tibet, Bulletin of Tibetology, Vol. 7, No. 2, 1970, pp. 39-40.
36. Cf; Jackson, D.P; The 'Miscellaneous Series' of Tibetan Texts in the Bihar Research Society, Patna, A. Handlist, Stultgart, 1989, Nos. 1278-1, -2 and -3.
37. Cf; / *bal-po'i-paṇḍita-chen-po-sgra-parnams-kyi-gtsug-gi-nor-lta-bu-bram-ze-chen-po-dze-ta-ka-rṇṇa-zhal-sṅa-nas-legs-par-mñan-te* / [Pek. 36v3].

38. Ibid
39. Cf;*/ lo-tsa-ba-śākya'i-dge-slon-ñi-ma-rgyal-mtshan-dpal-bzaṅ-pos /dpal-thar-pa-gliṅ-gi-gtsug-lag-khaṅ-du-legs-par-bsgyur-ba'o //* [Pek. 36 v3-4]
40. Cf; *bkra-śis-pa'i-dge-mtshan-du-ma-daṅ-ldan-pa'i-gnas / śel-dkar-gyi-gtsug-lag-khaṅ-du /* [Pek. 365 r 5-6].
41. The transllator was a student of śes-rab-seṅ-ge (1251-1315) and the teacher of Bu-ston rin-chen-grub (1290-1364). It is also know from the 'Blue Annals' (pp. 282-283) that from 1305 to 1312 our translator was abbot at *snar-thaṅ* monastery. Thus, we may suggest that he was flourshed in betwen last half of 13th century and first half of 14th century A.D.
42. Cf; Liebich, B; [ed] Cāndra-vṛtti, Leipzig, 1918, p. 23.
43. Cf; Ibid.
44. Cf; *ḱgra-chen-po-paṇḍita-dze-ta-karṇṇa'i-zhal-sṅa-nas-legs-par-mñan-te /lo-tsa-ba-śākya'i-dge-sloṅ-ñi-ma-rgyal-mtshan-dpal-bzaṅ-pos / dpal-thar-pa-gliṅ-gi-gtsug-lag-khaṅ-du-legs-par-bsgyur-ba'o //* [Pek. 41 r 8-V1].
45. Cf;*legs-par-sbyar-ba-sam-skṛta'i-tshul-cuṅ-zad-khoṅ-du-chud-pa'i-śākya'i-dge-sloṅ-ñi-ma-rgyal-mtshan-dpal-bzaṅ-pos // dpal-'byor-bu-ma-la-dbaṅ-thob-ciṅ- / brtse-ba-daṅ-dul-ba-la-sogs-pa-byaṅ-chub-sems-dpa'i-yon-tan-gyi-chos-daṅ-ldan-pa'i-slob-dpon-lha'i-sku-mkhar-gdud-phubs-su-bsgyur-ba'o //*[Pek. 42 V3-4]
46. It has been stated in the concluding phrase of the work that the work bears 119 ślokas Cf; Pek. 47 V8-48 r 1 (below) and Co. 42 r4.
47. Cf; */ brda-sprod-pa-tsāndra-pa'i-yi-ge'i-mdo'i-'grel-pa-ślo-ka-brgya-bcu-pa-rdzogs-so // // slob-dpon-chos-skyoṅ-gis-mdzad-pa'o /*[Pek. 47 v8-48 r1].
48. Refer th colophon of the work CH III/19, Pek. 293 V7.
49. Refer the colophon, Pek. 48 r1-3.
50. Ibid.
51. Cf;*/bal-po'i-mthil-ye-raṅ-gi-groṅ-khyer-du-dge-sloṅ-dpal-ldan-blo-gros-brtan-pas-yaṅ-dag-par-bsgyur-ba'o //* [Pke. 58 V 7-8].
52. In the first chapter the following masculine (pumliṅga) words are dealt with: *vṛkṣa, agni, sakhi, pati, vāyu, kartṛ, go, rai, nau, rājan, śvan, yuvan, daṇḍin, pathin, bhagavat, śrimat, candramas, vidvas, tasthivas, pums, anaḍuḥ, prāñc, udañc, tiryañc, vyaghrapad, pad, hṛdaya, sadṛś, div, mṛd, ap.* [cf; Pek. bor5 to 67v4]
53. The scond seection is incorporated with the following words (feminine): *khaṭvā, kumārī, vadhū, śrī, bhrū, sudhī, gati,*

dhenu, nandṛ, vāc, kṣudh, bhrū, kilalpā, grāmaṇī, makhalū, gati, sampad, yoṣṭi, niśā and *dārā*, Cf: [Pek. 67v4 to 71r6]

54. Chapter three bears the words like *kula, vāri, vastu, śastṛ, dadhi, akṣi, sāman, ahan, carman, payas, sarpis, āyus, mahat* and *jagat*, Cf; [Pek. 74r8 to 74r8]
55. The fourth chapter is incorporated with the folowing stems: *sarva, sarvaka, viśva*, and *viśvaka, ubha* and *ubhaya, katara, katama, datara, itara, anya* and *anyaka, anyatara* and *anyataraka, tvad, nema* and *nemaka, sama* and *samaka, sima* and *simaka, pūrva* and *pūrvaka, para, apara, dakṣina, uttara, adhara, sva, antara, tyad, tad, yad, etad, adas, idam, eka, dvi, tri, catur, pañcan, ṣaṣ, saptan, aṣṭan, nava, daśsan, yuṣmad* and *asmad, bhavat* and *kim*, Cf; [74r8 to 82r1]
56. There are 106 examples; 32 in the section on masculine. 18 in feminine, 14 in neuter and 42 pronominal and numeral stems. Also refer notes 52 to 55 for details.
57. Refer Pek. 59 r1 to 2.
58. Refer Pek. 58 v8.
59. Cf; Das, S.C.; A Tibetan-English Dictionary, Calcutta, 1902, p. 857.
60. Cf; *yon-tan-mtha'-yas-pa-daṅ-ldan-pa-bla-ma-dam-pa-chos-kyi-rgyal-po'i-bka'-luṅ-gis /bho-ṭa-paṇḍi-ta-yis-bskul-ba-bzhin-du-bal-po'i-paṇḍita-dpal-sa-dbaṅ-po'i-zhal-sṅa-nas / bod-kyi-lo-tsa-ba-dge-sloṅ-śoṅ-blo-brtan-gyis-bal-po'i-mthil-du-bsgyur-ba'o //* [Pek. 82r2-3]
61. Cf; Roerich, G.N.; The Blue Annals (in 2 vols), Calcutta, 1949-1953, pp. 785-787.
62. There are ten sections and twenty sub-sections in the treatise:

1.1.	laṭ :	a-taṅ	'present indicative : active'.
1.2.	laṭ :	taṅ	'present indicative : medium'.
2.1.	liṭ :	a-taṅ	'perfect : active'.
2.2.	liṭ :	taṅ	'perfect : active'.
3.1.	luṭ :	a-taṅ	'peripharastic future : active'.
3.2.	luṭ :	taṅ	peripharastic future medium'.
4.1.	lṛṭ :	a-taṅ	'future : active'.
4.2.	lṛṭ :	taṅ	'future : medium'.
5.1.	loṭ :	a-taṅ	'imperative : active'.
5.2.	loṭ :	taṅ	'imperative : medium'.
6.1.	laṅ :	a-taṅ	'imperfect : active '.
6.2.	laṅ :	taṅ	'imperfect : medium'
7.1.	liṅ :	a-taṅ	'optative : active'
7.2.	liṅ :	taṅ	'optative :medium'
8.1.	āśir liṅ :	a-taṅ	'precative (Tib. *smon-pa'i-liṅ*) : active'.

8.2.	āśir liṅ :	taṅ	'precative : medium'
9.1.	luṅ :	a-taṅ	'aorist : active'
9.2.	luṅ :	taṅ	'aorist : medium'
10.1.	lṛṅ :	a-taṅ	'conditional : active'
10.2.	lṛṅ :	taṅ	conditional : medium'

[Pek. 83r4 to 88r5]

63. Cf; /*tiṅ'i-mtha'-rdzogs-so* // /*dpal-gyis-byed-pa-yin-no* /. It means: the treatise on the forms ending in tiṅ has now been completed. It is the work of Dpal [Pek. 88r3]
64. Cf; Cordier, P; Catalogu du Fonds Tibetain de la Bibliothe-gue Nationale 3e Partie: Index du Bstan-ḥgyur (Tibetain 180-332), Paris, 1915, p. 460.
65. Cf; /*bod-kyi-lo-tsa-ba-dge-sloṅ-dpal-ldan-blo-gros-brtan-pas* / *bal-po'i-yul-rol-pa'i-groṅ-khyer-du-bsgyar-ciṅ-zhus-te-gtan-la-phab-pa'o* // [Pek. 88r3-4]
66. Refer, Hasrato, B.J; History of Nepal, Hoshiarpur, 1970, p. 21.
67. Ibid, foot note-2.
68. Cf; *'brel-pa-mdor-bstan-pa-thun-moṅ-du-bstan-pa*, Pek. 88r5 to 89r5.
69. Cf; *ti-sogs-bstan-pa* (Skt. tyādi), Pek. 89r5-v1.
70. Cf; *kṛt-mdor bstan-pa*, Pek. 89v1-8.
71. Cf; *kā-ra-ka-mdor-bstan-pa*, Pek. 89v8-90v4.
72. Cf; *bsdu-ba-mdor-bstan-pa* (Skt. *samāsa*), Pek. 90v4-91r2.
73. Cf; *de-phan-mdor-bstan-pa* (Skt. *taddhita*), Pek. 91r4-7.
74. Refre, Raja, K.K. (Ed), New Catalogue Catalogorum (Vol. VII), Madras University, 1973, p.2. [Cāṅgu or Caṅgadāsa]. We have also a second copy of this in orissa state Museum, BBSR.
75. Refr, Abhyankar, .V., and Shukla, J.M; A Dictionary of Sanskrit grammar, Baroda, 1987, p. 407. Also refer the *Kāśika* on P. III/4/1.
76. Bhartṛhari's Vākyapadīya contains the chapter *Sambandhasamuddeśa.* Also, refer, Cardona, G; Pāṇini a Survey of Research , pp. 301-302.
77. Refer the colophon of the treatise, Pek. 91r4-7 and co. 78r4-5.
78. (1) *phu (=bhū?)* la-sogs-pa-rnams [993 roots].
    (2) *ad-la-sogs-pa.* [69 roots]
    (3) *dzu-ho-ti-la-sogs-pa-rnams* [23 roots]
    (4) *di-ba-la-sogs-pa-rnams* [142 roots]
    (5) *su-la-sogs-pa-rnams* [26 roots]
    (6) *tud-* [149 roots]
    (7) *ru-dha-la-sogs-pa-rnams* [24 roots]
    (8) *ta-na-la-sogs-pa-rnams* [8 roots]

(9) *kṛ-la-sogs-pa-rnams* [56 roots]
(10) *tsu-ra-la-sogs-pa-rnams* [128 roots]

79. Refer, Palsule, G.B; The Sanskrit Dhātupāṭhas—A Critical Study, Poona, 1961, pp. 41-42.
80. Ibid; pp. 41 and 116.
81. Ibid; pp. 115-116.
82. For example we have 1944 roots in the *Siddhānta Kaumudī*, Ed. Pansikar, W.L.S. (Ed); *Siddhānta-Kaumudī* or Bhaṭṭojī Dīkṣhit's Vṛtti on Pāṇini's Vyākaraṇasūtras; Bombay, 1913, pp. 463-482.
83. In the ten *gaṇas* the number of roots are 993+69+23+142+26+149+24+8+56+128 [= 1618] respectively. Refer also the *bstan-'gyur*, [Pek. 435r7 to 446v7].
84. Cf; // *śākya'i-dge-sloṅ-rin-chen-grub-kyis-bsgyur-ciṅ-zhus-te-gtan-la-phab-pa'o* // //*yi-ge-pa-ni-yo-ga-ba-grub-pa-dpal-bzaṅ-po'o* //. It means the monk Śākya (-muni's order) *rin-chen-grub* has translated revised and estalihsed in a definite verson (of this work). The copyist was *yo-ga-pa grub-pa-dpal-bzaṅ-po.*
85. Cf; Rugg. D.S; The life of *bu-ston rin po che,* with the Tibetan Text of the *bu ston rnam thar,* Roma, 1966, p. 81: 11a4-11a7.
86. Ibid, p. 149; 37a7.
87. *Gshon-nu dpal* in his work *Deb-ther Sñon-po* mentions the above fact. Cf; Roerich, G.N. (Tra); The Blue Annals, Calcutta, 1949-1953, p. 785.
88. Cf; Co. 85v3.
89. Cf; *'di-ni-luṅ-ston-pa-tsāndra-pa'i-byiṅs-kyi-dpuṅ-gñen-slob-dpon-zla-ba-gaṅ-bas-mdzad-pa-las-btus-te- /dpal-e-chos-'byuṅ-ba'i-gtsug-lag-khaṅ-chen /por /lo-tsā-ba-thugs-rje-dpal-bzaṅ-pos-dga'-ba-zhes-pa-chu-pho-'brug-gi-lo'i-tha-skar-gyi-zla-ba-ñer-bzhi'i-ñin /skar-ma-rgyal-daṅ-gzá-phur-bu-jam-pa'i-grub-sbyor-bzaṅ-por-rdzogs-par-bsgyur-ba'o* /Cf; [Co. 85v3-4].
90. Cf; // *legs-par-sbyar-ba'i-skad-kyi-brda-sprod-pa'i-bstan-bcos-slob-dpon-chen-po-tsāndra-go-mis-mdzad-pa'i rjes-su-'braṅs-te* /[Co. 114r4].
91. Refer the colophon i.e. Co. 114r4 to v1.
92. Ibid.
93. Cf; Khetsun Sangpo; Biographical Dictionary of Tibet and Tibetan Buddhism, Dharmasala, (in 11 vols).
94. Ibid, p. 194.
95. Ibid, p. 199.
96. Refer Co. 152r5 for colophon.
97. Ibid.

98. Refer the colophon for details.
99. Cf; Liebich, B; (ed); Cāndra-vyākaraṇa ... er. Lipzing, 1902, pp. IX-X.
100. Cf; // *brda'-sprod-pa-tsāndra-pa'i-mdo'i-byiṅs-kyi-tshogs-kyi-gleg-bam-gyi-mdo / slob-dpon-gaṅ-ba'i-zla-ba'i-zhabs-kyis-mdzad-pa-rdzogs-so* //[Pek. 322 V6]
101. Cf; New Ct. Cat., vol. 9, 1977, pp. 287-89 for details.
102. Refer the Colophon, Pek. 447r5 to 460r8.
103. Cf; *na-mtha'-can.* masculine ending in 'n', Pek. 460r-8.
104. Cf; pek 460v3 to 464v3.
105. Cf; Pek 464v3 to 470v3.
106. Cf; Pek 470r3 - 5.
107. Cf; sṅon-bod-du-ma'gyur-snaṅ-bas; Pek. 293v8.
108. According to the colophon: "This text has been written by the master Candragomin personally, who has acquired perfct accomplishments and who is covered by the unique unstained white parasol of prfect fame in this world, viz., *'di-ni-'dzam-bu'i-gliṅ-mthá-dag-sñan-grags-kyi-gdugs-dkar-po-dri-ma-med-pa-gcig-gis-khebs-pa-dṅos-grab-mchog-brñes-pa'i-slob-dpon-tsāndra-go-mai'i-zhal-sṅa-nas-mdzad-pa-ste* / [Pek. 293v7-v8]
109. Cf; *'dzin-byed-ces-bya-ba-me-pho-byi-ba'i-rgyal-can-gyi-ña-la* [Pek. 294r1[.
110. Cf; *kha-ra-zhes-bya-ba-lcags-mo-yos-kyi-dboi'i-zla-ba'i-dkar-phyogs-kyi-rgyal-ba-gñis-pa-la* [Pek. 294r3].

4

KĀTANTRA SYSTEM OF SANSKRIT GRAMMAR

History of Kalāpa system of grammar (Indian tradition):

In the post-pāṇinian period, a number of scholars had composed their glosses to avoid a large and difficult work like the Aṣṭ of Pāṇini. The Kalāpa system of Śarvavarman is oldest among them. This system of Śarvavarman is also known as the Kātantra system and as the Kaumāra system. According to the statement of Trilocanadāsa, the noted grammarian, the word *Kātantra* means "a small work" and the work so termed because of its being a very short and simple work so termed because of its being a very short and simple work in Sanskrit grammar.[1] It is also called Kalāpa or Kaumāra; because its author Śarvavarman is said, according to a tradition, to have obtained the sūtras constituting it from the quill *(Kalāpa)* of the peacock of Kumāra i.e. Kārtikeya, the son of Śiva.

Like many historical figures, the personal history of Śarvavarman is problematical. Neither the author himself, nor his contemporaries have given any information regarding his personal life or history. It is known from a work of early mediaeval period that Śarvavarman was a Brāhmin Paṇḍit from south and was a minister of the king Sātavāhana.[2] This information regarding the age of the author rather confuses us to determine the exact date of Śarvavarman. In the history of India there were a number of Śātavāhana kings who ruled over mainly the Deccan region, south India and Malwa region. Further, a 11th century text suggests that Śarvavarman and Guṇāḍhya were in a court of Sātavāhana of Malwa region.[3] If it is true then the work was composed around the beginning of the Christian era.[4] S.K.

Belvalkar suggests that our author was flourished in the 1st century A.D. He, however, gives not sufficient arguments in support of his statement.[5]

In keeping with the motivations to brevity and simplicity, the Kātantra sūtras return to the older method of ordering the syllables (as found in the Prātiśākhyas), arrange discussions of things more naturally (similarly to the arrangement later adopted within the Pāṇinian tradition by Dikṣita in his Siddhāntakaumudī), and omits many of the most difficult rules prescribed by Pāṇini. The result is a work of 1,765 sūtras6 with four sections only, in contrast to Pāṇini's four thousand. The four sections *(adhyāyas)* deals with technical terms, *samdhi sūtras,* declension syntax, compounds, taddhita conjagation, voice and verbal derivatives in an order.

The earliest commentator on the sūtras of Śarvavarman was Durgasimha, who was flourished around 7th century A.D. Writers subsequent to Durgasimha have mainly confined themselves to writing sub-commentaries on the masterly commentary *(vṛtti).* The earliest of these is the Kātantravistara by Vardhamāna, whose patron was Karṇadeva, a king, who ruled over Gujrat in 11th century A.D. Then Trilocanadāsa had composed the Kātantravṛṭtipañjikā, which is a scholarly work in the Kātantra system.

History of Kalāpa system of grammar (Tibetan tradition):

The second of the two most prominent Sanskrit grammatical systems in Tibet is the Kalāpa system. It is said earlier that this system was founded by Sarvavarman. However, the Tibetans call the author as Śarvavarma and Saptavarma. While *Bu-ston rin-chen-grub* calls the author Sarvavarma,[7] both Tāranātha and *Koṅ-sprul blo-gros-mtha'-yas* suggests that Saptavarma[8] was the founder of this system.

Further Tā. catagorically states that Saptavarma, translated as *bdun-pa'i-go-cha* 'seven-armour',[9] is the correct form. Iśvaravarma[10] and Sarvavarma are erroneous forms of his name. Indeed, in the Tibetan Literature, the author of the Kātantra sūtras has been given quite a few different names or viz., Saptamvarma, Sarvavarma and Iśvarvarma.[11]

A beautiful story is found about this grammar in the Kathāsaritsāgara[12] and in the Bṛhatkathāmañjarī the above story has been represented briefly.[13] Like the Indian tradition, we have the legend in the Tibetan tradition also. However, in the Tibetan tradition the story differs slightly. Ko. gives a summary of the legend, whereas Bu, and Tā give a more elaborate version. It describes how a king variously named Sātavāhana (in the Kathāsaritsāgara), Udayana (Bu. and Ko.) or Śaṅkara (Ta), displayed a lack of knowledge of Sanskrit grammar. While the king was bathing along with his wives, his ignorance comes to light. During the playing in the water one queen says to the king: *modakair deva paritāḍaya mām* (Kathāsaritsāgara) 'Oh king, do not sprinkle me with water'; *modakam dehi* (Bṛhatakathāmañjarī); or *ma modakaiḥ siñca* (Tibetan tradition, with emendation) "Do not sprinkle me with water". But, not recognizing the form *modaka*—to be a *samdhi* combination of *mā* + *udaka* ('not' + 'water'), the king ordered for the sweetmeats *(modakas)*. After this the queen laughed at the king and strongly urged him to study Sanskrit grammar as his earliest. Then the king ordered to compose a short manual that would enable him to apprehend Sanskrit grammar in a short time. Śarvavarman, one of his ministers agreed to help him to learn the said grammar within six-months through a short treatise and thus, Śarvamarman composed the Kātantra sūtras.

It is also known that by the grace of his tutelory deity Kārttikeya (Kumāra or Ṣaṇmukha) [Bu. *gzhon-nu-smin-drug;* Tā and Ko: *gzhon-nu-gdoṅ-drug*] he was able to prepare such a grammar. According to the Tibetan sources, the deity merely uttered. '*siddho varnasamāmnāyaḥ*' i.e. Kātantra sūtra No. I-1-1, after which all grammar in a synoptic form was clear to Śarvavarman.

The original text is supposed to have consisted of four chapters of four sub-chapters in each. Later the last two chapters were merged and a new chapter on *kṛt* suffixes was added by another grammarian, variously identified as Vararuci, Kātyāyana and Śākaṭāyana. More additions, some in verse form, were inserted in the other chapters to cover secondary derivation *(taddhita suffixes)*, nominal composition and feminine nominal suffixes.

The state of the *Kātantra sūtra* text on which Durgasimha composed his *vṛtti* is identical to the one found in the Tibetan canonical translation of this sūtra text (CH IV/2). It represents the second stage of the development of this text. It has four chapters on (i) *samdhi* (5 sub-chaptres), (ii) nominal declension (2.1 to 2.3), case syntax and case semantics (2.4), nominal composition (2.5) and secondary nominal derivations (2.6) [six sub-chapters] (iii) verbal conjugation (eight sub-chapters) and (iv) primary nominal derivations (six sub-chapters).

The most extensive version of the *Kātantra* is exemplified by the commentary entitled *Śiṣyahitā,* only known in the Tibetan version (CH IV/5 and also CH IV/3). Here the four chapters respectively consist of six, seven, eight and six sub-chapters, which is possibly typical of a Kashmiri tradition. This development of the text is integrated into the legend by Bu. According to him Kārtikeya expounded the grammar up to the fifteenth sub-chapters. This would correspond to the oldest vision of sixteen pādas. In this state the work did not deal with all the necessary aspects of grammar, so Śarvavarma (as Bu. calls him) and Vararuci wrote additional sub-chapters to this. The text then consisted of twentyfour sub-chapters, amounting to four hundred verses. The number of twentyfour sub-chapters could correspond to the second version, as represented by the Tibetan sūtra-text (CH IV/1) or the text commented upon by Durgasimha (cf; CH IV/2), either with or without sub-chapters 2.5 and 2.6.[14]

Tā. remarks that an older tradition has it that Kārttikeya only dictated a part of the text, but he does not mention the later additions any or other authors than Saptavarma (as Tā. calls him). Tā. remarks that according to a chronicle *kumāra-ṣaṇmukha* explained the treatise up to the fourth pāda of the section on the verb of the Kalāpa grammar.15 If Tā. thinks that the oldest version ended at the fourth sub-chapter of the chaptper on verbs, this would mean a version over shorter than the ones proposed so far.

Further, Bu. mentions Paṇḍit *grags-'byor* wrote a commentary entitled "Beneficient for the students" viz., *Paṇḍit-grags-'byor-gyis-'grel-pa-slob-ma-la-phan-pa-zhes-byas-so* / This refers to the volumnous *Śiṣyahitā* commentary by Ugrabhūti, which has been preserved in Tibetan translation, one complete of almost three hundred follies (viz. CH IV/5) and one excerpt (viz. CH IV/3).

Ko. mentions treatises on *sy-ādi* i.e. nominal declension [CH IV/6] and *ty-ādi* i.e. verbal conjugation [CH IV/8]. Again Ko.

states that *śoṅ-ston rdo-rje-rgyal-mtshan* and *dpaṅ blo-gros-brtan-pa* as the first Tibetan translators of treatise on the *Kātantra* system.

Works:

CH IV/1: Tib. *ka-lā-pa'i-mdo*
"Sūtras of Kalāpa"
[Pek. 5775, Nā. 3767, De. 4292, Co. LE 1]
Skt.: Kalāpa sūtrāṇi
Author: Śarvavarma (De. *rgyal-po'i lha*)
Translator/s: *blo-gros-brtan-pa-gsum-pa.*
Place: *sa-skya.*
Date: 14th century A.D.

It has been mentioned earlier that the basic text of the Kalāpa or Kātantra or Kaumāra system of Sanskrit grammar consists of sūtras concerning morphology, morphophonemics and semantics of classical Sanskrit. The present treatise is divided into four chapters dealing with *Samdhi,* nominal forms, verbal forms and primary nominal derivatives respectively. These four chapters are, further, sub-divided into five, six, eight and six *pādas* (Tib. *rkaṅ-pa*)

This is also the form of the *sūtra*-text as commented upon by Durgasimha in his *vṛtti* which is the basic *Kātantra* commentary. But this seems not have been the oldest forms of the text. There are good reasons to assume that the whole fourth section and *padas* five and six of the second section (i.e. 2.5 and 2.6) are later additions.

Traditionally the original Sanskrit text of the Kātantra grammar is attributed to Sarvavarman, a famous grammarian, about whom no reliable historical information is available (our study suggests that he was flourished just before the chirstian era).

As far as methodology, presentation and ordering of the sūtras are concerned this system is more divergent from Pāṇini than Cāndra is: the generative method (in effect rather a 'Substitutive' method), typical for Pāṇini as well as for Cāndra, is often replaced in Kātantra by constrastive tabulation, e.g. of various paradigms. Compare e.g. Kā. III-1-24 to 33, on the verbal tenses and moods, with the treatment in Pāṇini of the same topic viz., P. III-4-78 to 117.

There are no Śiva-sūtras[16] at the beginning of this grammar, as we find in Pāṇini and in a slightly variant forms in the Cāndra system of grammar. Again, it is to mark that in this grammar Śarvavarman uses the traditional order of the alphabet when referring to the group of phonemes.[17] An other important characteristic feature of this grammar is the technical metalinguistic use of the cases. Pāṇini and Cāndra prescribe many grammatical, particularly morphophonemic, operations in the form of a substitution where the substitutied gets genitive case and the substitute nominative case, where as this system uses a different prescriptive method, viz. in the form of a change, where the element to be changed gets nominative case and the prescribed result of the transformation accusative case.[18]

However, in some cases this system is closer to Pāṇini's grammar than the Cāndra grammar: e.g. in the use of many terms in the technical vocabulary that are known from Pāṇinian system, but that Cāndra avoids using.

In the colophon of the work it has been mentioned that this work had been translated in the monastery called *sa-skya* by (gsum-pa-yis) *blo-gros-brtan-pa* on the basis of the commentary by Durgasimha.[19] It is known to all the scholars that Durgasimha had prepared his commentary on the Kalāpa sūtras and that is the best commentary available now.

During the early 1930s, M. Lalou has suggested that our translator i.e., *blo-gros-brtan-pa* is identical with a great scholar called *grags-pa-rgyal-mtshan.*[20] However, this identification is not fully correct Lalou's suggestion is based on the fact that while this text refers to *blo-gros-brtan-pa* as the translator in the dkar-chag of the Peking *bstan-'gyur grags-pa-rgyal-mtshan* is stated to be the translator of the text. Moreover, the colophon of the text (the translation found in the Peking and *snar-thaṅ* edition) refers to *blo-gros-brtan-pa* as translator and the Peking *dkar-chag* refers *grags-pa-rgyal-mtshan* as the translator. Therefore, Lalou argues that both are same.

The text Kalāpa *sūtra-vṛtti* is extant in two versions in the various *bstan-'gyur* redactions. *Co-ne* and *sde-dge* have a separate version (see CH IV/2) and Peking and Snar-thaṅ have another version. While the former contains the first section and the first sub-section of the second one upto sūtra no 41, the later contains the same translation with minor variations, mainly of orthographical nature. Again, it is supplemented with a translation of the remaining sūtras of the first sub-section of the second one i.e. 40 to 77. In the former we find that *grags-pa-rgyal-mtshan* as the translator and the colophon of the later mentions *blo-gros-brtan-pa* as the translator. Thus, we may suggest the identification of Lalou is not conclusive.

Sa-skya was a well-known monastary of the *sa-skya-pa* sect and it was situated in the southern part of the *gtsaṅ* province, some one hundred kilometres to the south-east of *gzhis-ka-rtse*.[21] It was founded in 1073 A.D. by *khon dkon-mchog-rgyal-po* and in the later age it became a main centre for Sanskrit studies. A large number of Tibetan and Sanskrit mss. are preserved in this monastry.[22]

CH IV/2 Title *cha-bsags-kyi-mdo'i-grel-pa (-zhes-bya-ba)*
"Commentary on the Sūtras of Kalāpa"
[De-4283, Co. LE 2]
Skt. Kalāpa-sūtra-nāma-vṛtti.
Author: Durgasimha
Translator/s: *grags-pa-rgyal-mtshan*
Place: Not mentioned
Date: 14th century A.D.

This treatise is a commentary on the *Ka-lā-pa'i-mdo* composed by Durgasimha during 7th century A.D. However, the Tibetan translation of the Durgasimha's *vṛtti* is incomplete. It covers only the first major section on *saṃdhi* and part of the first *pāda* (upto and including Kā. II-1.41) of the second section. It has been identified in the list of grammatical treatises in the 14th century canonical catalogues with the present translation by *grags-pa-rgyal-mtshan,* that occurs only in the *Co-ne* and *sde-dge* editions of the *bstan-'gyur.* The translation as found in the Peking (5776) and snar-thaṅ (3738) editions, attributed to *blo-gros-brtan-pa,*[23] is presumably related to the present translation, as they correspond closely: in fact they are virtually identical bar slight variations, mainly orthographical-up to sūtra Kā. II-1-41. But the work found in the Peking and Snar-thaṅ editions include more of the text: it contains the commentary on the first section and the whole of the first sub-section of the second one[24] i.e. upto the Kā. II-1-77. Besides, among the Sanskrit palm leaf mss. described by Sāṅkṛtyāyana (1930 A.D.) we find one incomplete ms. of Durgasimha's *vṛtti* in the collection of *Ṅör* monastery.

It has been mentioned in the translation of *blo-gros-brtan-pa* that he had consulted the sub-commentary of Trilocanadāsa, for the translation, as the basic work.[25] However, no Tib. trans. of the sub-commentary of Trilocanadāsa is available; but Sāṅkṛtyāyana had founded three complete work of this sub-commentary in the library of *sa-skya* monastery. It should be noted that this same redaction of the *sūtra*-text as met with in Durgasimha's *vṛtti*, consisting of sub-chapters five, six, eight and six *pādas* respectively, served as basis for two major *Kātantra*-commentaries that were originally written in Tibetan, viz., one by *bu-ston rin-chen-grub* (14th century) and the other by the *sa-skya-pa scholar sa-bzaṅ-ma-ti-paṇ-chen (blo-gros-rgyal-mtshan)* 14th century A.D.)

Refer CH IV/1 for the author.

In the ms. the place of translation is not mentioned by the translator.

CH IV/3

Title: *Ka-lā-pa'i grel-pa-ñuṅ-ṅu-las-slob-ma-la-phan-pa (.zhes-bya-ba)*

:Short commentary on Kalāpa for benefit of the student".

[Pek. 5777, Nā. 3769, De. 4284 and Co. LE 3]

Skt. Kalāpa-laghu-vṛtti-śiṣyahitā (-nāma)

Author: *grags-'byor* / *sgrol-ba'i dbaṅ-phyug*

Translator/s *lha-bla-ma-zhi-ba-'od*

Place: *gser-gyi-gtsug-lag-khaṅ* in *tho-liṅ* in *zhaṅ-zhuṅ*

Date: 11th century A.D. (2nd half)

This is a work on Kātantra system of grammar and it covers only the verbal morphology portion i.e. Kā. III-1-1 to Kā. III-4-123. It is in fact an excerpt from an extensive commentary on Kātantra grammar i.e. the *śiṣyahitā* commentary (Refer CH IV/6) by Ugrabhuti, an integral translation of which occurs in the Tibetan canon too.

It is a notable feature of the present translation that it often quotes the sūtras in Sanskrit before translating them into Tibetan. No Sanskrit ms. of this work—neither a part nor in complete—seems to have been preserved. The name of the author of this commentary is given in variant forms in Tibetan viz., *drag-byor* and *grags-byor,* and has consequently restricted into Sanskrit as Ugrabhuti, Rudrabhuti, (both for *drag-byor*); 'Yaśobhuti, Kirtībhuti (both for *grags-byor).* Here Ugrabhuti seems the most plausible restoration, as this name is found in Indian sources in connection with this commentary.[27]

Sgrol-ba'i dbaṅ-phyug is given as the name of the compiler of the treatise under discussion.[28] Several Sanskrit reconstructions have been proposed for this Tibetan name. Such as Muktanātha or Muktasvāmin Tārānātha, Tārakeśvara or Tāreśvara. But no conclusive evidence seems to be avilable.

The work was translated by *lha-bla-ma zhi-ba-od,* a sound scholar from Western Tibet in the second half of 11th century and it is the earliest datable translation of a Sanskrit grammatical treatise in the corpus of 14th century *bstan-'gyur.*[29]

The section on verb (i.e. the present text) of the Kalāpa system is divided into four sub-sections (pādas) [Pek. 152 v2 to 165 v5].

The place of translation was *gser-gyi-gtsug-lag-khaṅ* 'Golden Temple' of *tho-liṅ.* It was in the country of *zhaṅ-zhuṅ,* the ancient Western Tibetan Kingdom. Its central province was *guge.*[30]

CH IV/4

Title: *Ka-lā-pa'i-'grel-pa*
"Commentary on Kalāpa (grammar)
[BD, 13, SD. 13]
Skt: Kalāpavṛtti
Author: Durgasimha
Tanslator/s: *bu-ston (rin-chen-gurb).*
Place: Not mentioned
Date: 14th century A.D.

The translation of this work was done by *bu-ston riṅ-chen-grub* (1290-1364) and this is not preserved in the extant xylographic editions of the *bstan-'gyur.* It is the only title within the earliest Tibetan corpus on Sanskrit grammar as described in the two 14th century *dkar-chags*, that cannot be identified with a treatise in 18th century editions of the Tibetan canon.

It is to mark that in the *dkar-chag* (Eng. Index) to the Co-ne *bstan-'gyur* reference to this treatise can be found, viz., as fifth in Volume LE of *mdo-grel* section,[31] but the text is not actually included in the Co-ne edition.

Again it is not out of context to mention here that *bu-ston* himself has written an extensive sub-commentary on the Kātantra grammar (Refer CH IV/2 and CH IV/4). However, it is not clear if there is any relation between *bu-ston's* commentary and the present work in 14th century catalogues.

Bu-ston (1290-1364) was a famous scholar. He had contributed three translations to the earliest corpus of Sanskrit grammatical literature in Tibetan.[32] It is known from his biography [written by his pupil *sgra-tshad-pa rin-chen-rnam-rgyal* (1318-1388)] that in 1310s he studied Sanskrit grammar, Lexicography and paleography under *thar-pa-lo-tsā-bañi-ma-rgyal-mtshan* for more than four years.,[33] particularly there he had acquired knowledge on Cāndra and Kātantra system of Sanskrit grammar.

The translation of the present text (Durga's commentary on Kātantra), which has not been preserved in the xylographic editions of the *Bstan-'gyur*, must have ben made prier to 1335 (composition of the *dkar-chag*). In the biography it has been mentioned that abound 1344 he had translated the 'remainder' of Durga's Kātantra commentary.[34] Besides the present work he had translated two other texts i.e. CH III/9 and CH IV/7. However, both of these works are concerned with the dhātupāṭhas.

As, it has been mentioned on the biography that he had translated the 'remainder' of Durga's commentary in 1344, we may safely suggest that the work was translated in 14th century A.D. The place of translation has not been mentioned in the colophon.

CH IV/5

Title *luṅ-ston-pa ka-lā-pa'i-mdo'i-grel-pa-slob-ma-la-phan-pa (-zhes-bya-ba).*

"Commentary on the Kalāpa sūtras entitled śiṣyahitā"

[Pek. 5884, Nā. 3876, De. 4286, Co. LE 5]

Skt. Kalāpa-vyākaraṇa-sūtra-śiṣyahitā nāma.
Author Ugrabhuti (Tib. *grag-byor-seś-rab / grags-byor-śes-rab / drag-'byor).*
Translator/s: *dpaṅ blo-gros-brtan-pa.*
byaṅ-chub-rtse-mo.
Copyist: *rig-pa'i-rgyal-po and blo-gros-dpal.*
Place: *phrul-snaṅ, guṅ-thaṅ, e-chos-'byuṅ* and *dwags-po-rdzam-yul,*
Date: 14th century A.D.

This is an extensive sub-commentary on the whole text of the Kātantra system of grammar, presumably dating from 10th century.[35]

On the various forms of the author's name, (cf; CH IV/3), the portion *śes-rab* in his name is generally ignored in the Sanskrit rendering: strictly speaking Ugrabhutiprajñā should be considered as a plausible reconstruction too.

The redaction of the *sūtra*-text as commented upon in this *śiṣyahitā* commentary is different from that in Durga's *vṛtti.*[36] In the present commentary the first section as well as the second section contain one *pāda* more than in Durga's *vṛtti.* These later additions are sub-sections I.6 (an *samdhi* of particles) and II.7 (on derivation of feminine nouns)[37] these accretions are perhaps typical of a Kashmiri tradition.[38]Thus, in the present treatise we have four major sections, consisting of six, seven, eight and six sub sections respectively. It should be noted that precisely one of the two *pādas* that are later additions, viz., *pāda* 2.7 (on derivation of feminine nouns) is dealt with in a separate section in a well-known 18th Century Sanskrit-Tibetan lexicon, the so-called Prajñā dictionary, written by the *sa-skya-pa* Lāmā *bstan-'dzin-rgyal-mtshan.*[39]

The whole text was not translated by a single person in one place. It is known from the colophon at the end of the 2.1 that "this part of the text has been translated by *dpal-ldaṅ blo-gros-brtan-pa* and the copyist was *rig-pa'i-rgyal-pa.*[40]

The second and third sub-sections of the second section was translated by *byaṅ-chub-rtse-mo* in , *'Phrul-snaṅ'* temple at Lhasa.[41]

The 4th, 5th and 6th sub-sections of the second section of the text have been translated by *byaṅ-chub-rtse-mo* in the monastic academy of *E-chos-'byuṅ.*[42] The 7th sub-section of this section was translated by the same person at *dags-po rdzam-yul.*

The chapter on verbal forms (si-sogs) of the commentary called *śiṣyahitā* i..e the full 3.1 and some portion of 3.2 have been translated by *dpal-ldaṅ blo-gros-brtan-pa* and the copyist of this portion was *blo-gros-dpal.* The rest of the 3rd chapter was translated by *byaṅ-chub rtse-mo*[43] and the 1st sub-section of the 4th chapter (i.e 4.1) has been translated by *dpaṅ to-tsa-ba blo-gros-brtan-pa.*[44] The rest of the treatise has been translated in *dwags-po rdzam-yul* by *byaṅ-chub-rtse-mo* with the grace of *dpal-ldaṅ blo-gros-brtan-pa.*[45]

Thus, the whole text has been translated by two translators in four different places.

dpaṅ blo-gros-brtan-pa (From last quarter of 13th century to 1st half of 14th century A.D.) was one of the main exponents of Sanskrit Linguistics in Tibet. Refer CH III/5 for his life and works.

Byaṅ-chub-rtse-mo (14th century A.D.) was the nephew and pupil of *dpaṅ blo-gros-brtan-pa.* It is said that he met *tsoṅ-kha-pa.* His chief disciple was *nam-mkha'-bzaṅ-po,* who has translated CH III/15, CH IV/11 and CH VII/5 during 14th century A.D. Our translator is said to have contributed five translations to the *bstan-'gyur,* one in the *tantra* section, four in the *sūtra* section. Among the later four, beside the two translations CH III/14 and CH IV/5, we find two translations he worked on in collaboration with his disciple *nam-mkha'-bzaṅ-po,* viz., a treatise on prosody entitled *chandaratnākara* and the remarkable translation of one of the masterpieces of Indian *Kāvya* literature, viz., the *Meghaduta* of Kālidāsa.

Phrul-snaṅ (-gtsug-lag-khaṅ) is the ancient name of the famous *jo-khaṅ* of *lhāsa.*

Guṅ-thaṅ may be identified as the monastery *mtshal* (or *tshal) guṅ-thaṅ,* located some ten k.ms. to the east of Lhasa, on the opposite side of *skyid-chu* river. *Mtshal* is the name of the district, *guṅ-thaṅ* is the name of the monastery founded in 1175, which became the base of the *mtshal-pa* sub-sect of the *bka'-brgyud-pa.*

E-chos-'byuṅ (-gi-gtsug-lag-khaṅ) is the name of an ancient monastery. But its identification has some problems. The monastery of the *ṅor-pa* sub-sect of the *sa-skya-pa* sect i.e. *nor e-wam* may be in identified with this. However, this was founded by *kun-dga'-bzaṅ-pa* in 1429. Thus, it is not possible to suggest that before 1335 (date of compilation of *Bu-ston's dkar-chag)* a translation of Sanskrit work was made there. Unless we consider this part of CH IV/5 which was translated in *e-chos-'byuṅ* (viz., 2.4 to 2.6) as a later addition to the canon we cannot but conclude that another monastery must be intended here.

The location of the monastery—*dwags-po rdzam-yul* is not exactly identified. However, *dwags-po* is a well-known toponym which has been identified as the region to the south of the river *gtsaṅ-po* and to the east of *rtse-thaṅ,* to the south-east of *dbus* province, perhaps partly applying also to some adjacent areas north of the *gtsaṅ-po* river.

Thus, *byaṅ-chub-rts-mo* had translated the work in four places. However, it is not known from the colophon that where *blo-gros-brtan-pa* had translated the work with the help of two copyists i.e. *rig-pa'i-rgyal-po and blo-gros-dpal.*

CH IV/6:

Title: *si-la-sogs-pa-mthai-bya-ba*
"Technical derivations ending in 'si' etc."
[Pek. 5778, Nā 3770, De, 4287 and Co. SE 1]
Skt: si-ādy-anta-prakriyā
Author: *Mañju kirtī* (Tib. *jam-dpal-grags-pa /jam-pa'i-grags-pa)*
Translator/s: *dpal-ldan blo-gros-brtan-pa*
dpaṅ blo-gros-brtan-pa.
Place: *dpal gnas-po-che*
Date: 14th century A.D.

This is a work with four sections. It contains a study on nominal declensions according to the Kātantra system of grammar. The first section bears the sūtras relating to masculine nouns and chapter two is concerned with neuter nouns. The third chapter is corroborated with feminine nouns and declension of adjectives, pronouns and adjectives are dealt with in the last section. The first section and the third section has two subsections each-on stems ending in vowel and consonant respectively.[46] The last section contains four *pādas;* on adjectives ending in vowel, adjectives ending in consonant, pronouns and numerals respectively.[47] However, the second chapter has no sub-sections.[48]

It is a matter of regret that the original Sanskrit text of this translational work is not available at present. However Rahul Sāṅkṛtyāyana mentions a eight-eight leaf ms. under the title *Triliṅgaprakaraṇa.* According to his description, many Sanskrit palm-leaf manuscripts were kept in several monasteries with this title. In this ms. the name of the author has been mentioned as *Mañju.*[49] Thus, we may infer that this may be the basic text for the Tibetan translation.

Refer CH III/5 for the translator.

It is known from the colophon that this excellent work has been written by *Mañjukirtī,* who was a boatman on the Occan, with a voice of a Kinggoose on a lotuspond and who was the character of a lion, in an minent monastic academy.[50]

Due to the lack of evidences, it is not possible for us to identify *dpal gnas-po-che*,[51] where the monastic academy was situated. But, according to db-ther-sṅon-po, *dpaṅ blo-gros-brtan-pa* resided here for a long time.

CH IV/7:

Title: *dbyiṅs-ki-tshogs*
"Corpus of verbal roots"
[Pek. 5842, 3884, De. 4285, Co. LE4]
Skt. *Dhātu-kāya*
Author: Durgasimha *(bgrod-dka'-seṅ-ge)*
Translator/s: *bu-ston rin-chen-grub*
Place: Not mentioned
Date: First half of 14th Century A.D.
Copyist: *rin-chen-rnam-rgyal.*

In the colophon Durgasimha has been mentioned as the compiler of treatise[52] which is merely a catalogue of the 335 verbal roots. Durgasimha is known as an authority on the *dhātupāṭha* literature in general[53] and as the standard commentator of Kātantra grammar. Since the compiler of this work is Durgasimha, we may safely suggest that the present work belongs to Kātantra system of Sanskrit grammar. This view is further supported by the fact that one of the characteristic of the Kātantra system that is found here is the division of the roots into the nine major classes *(gaṇas)*, combining the elsewhere second and third classes into one, instead of ten as in Pāṇini and Cāndra.

The original Sanskrit form of the Kātantra's Dhātupāṭha (cf; Palsul, 1961, pp. 49-53) has not been edited. Therefore, it is not possible to suggest that the Tibetan version is identical with the *Kātantra-dhātupāṭha.* All the idiosyncracies of Durgasimha's *dhātupāṭha* mentioned by Palsule are met with in the present text (CH IV/7) e.g. the characteristic phrase introducing the sub-group of roots headed by *yuj,* in class X, is found in verbation translation.[54]

Refer CH III/4 for the translator.

CH IV/8:
Title: *ti-la-sogs-pa'i-mtha'i-bya-ba-rnam-par-dpyad-pa(-zhes-bya-ba).*
"Detailed expose of the technical derivation of the forms ending in *ti* etc."
[Pek. 5793, Nā. 3785, De. 4289 and Co. SE 3]
Skt: *ti-day-antasya prakriyā-vicārita-nāma.*
Author: Sarvadhara
Translator/s: *śoṅ-ston-rdo-rje-rgyal-mtshan.*
Place: *ṅam-riṅ-gi-yaṅ-rtse*
Date: Second half of 13th century A.D.

This is a voluminous treatise on verbal conjugations and it perhaps belongs to Kātantra system. Though it is a separate work, but it is very similar to the work CH IV/13 discussed below.

The work begins with a general introduction with an enumeration of the basic verbal endings. There are nineteen sections in the work and the first ten sections are concerned with the standard group of ten tenses and moods[55] and the other sections are incorporated with rules of various derivative verb forms.[56]

The first section is also divided into ten sub-section and the first nine deal with the ten different formations of the present indicative stem for active and medium, corresponding to the ten major classes of primitive verbal bases as listed in the *dhātupāṭhas* and the tenth sub-sections deals with passive conjugation.[57] The sūtras quoted in this work are similar to that of Kātantras.[58] However, the original Sanskrit work of the treatise does not seem to have been critically edited and we may identify this work with a palm-leaf ms. as described by Sāṅkṛtyāyana. According to Sāṅkṛtyāyaṇa, the work is written in *māgadhi* and has been kept in the ṅor e-wam-chos-sde monastory in central Tibet and belongs to Kalāpa system.[60]

Again the New Catalogue Catalogrum mentions a work entitled the *Tyādyantasyaprakriyā* which is ascribed to Sarvadhara Upādhyaya.[61] The same text is also called: *Kalapatyādivṛtti.*[62] Now we may suggest that the same text was translated into Tibetan and has been preserved.

Refer CH IV/4 for the translator.

The colophon describes that the work was translated at the monastic academy of noble *ṅam-riṅ-gi-yaṅ-rtse.*[63] The monastery *yaṅ-rtse* is not identified so-far. However, *ṅam-riṅ* is a region which is located on the north bank of *gtsaṅ-po* river opposite to *lha-rtse* and *phun-tshogs-gliṅ* (in the western part of *gtsaṅ* province).

CH IV/9

Title: *ka-lā-pa'i-mdo-daṅ-'brel (De.-grel)-ba'i-si-la-sogs-pa'i-rnam-dbye'i-bya-ba.*

"Derivations of the nominal cases *si* etc. according to *Kalāpa sūtras*"

[De. 4288 and Co. SE 2]

Skt.: *Kalāpasūtra-sambandha-syādi-vibhakti-prakriyā.*

Author: Mām-hi-ka-wi

Translator/s: *blo-gros-rgyal-mtshan* and *blo-gros-dpal-dzoṅ-po* (Based on instructions of *blo-gros-brtan-pa,* at the instigation of *chos-grags-dpal-bzaṅ-po). blo-gros-brtan-pa* and *chos-grags-dpal-bzaṅ-po* (De.).

Place: Not mentioned

Date: 14th century A.D.

This is a scholarly work on the nominal declensions and affiliated to the Kalāpa system. It has six sections dealing with masculine, neuter, feminine, adjectives pronomical declension and numerals. The first four sections are each divided into two sub-sections, dealing with stems ending in vowels and consonants respectively.[64]

A close study of this text suggests that the structure and method of the work are similar to those of CH IV/6's. Again we may opine that these two works i.e. CH IV/6 and CH IV/9 are the translations based on one identical Sanskrit work. However, according to the colophons the authors and translators are different. The author of the present treatise is a great Paṇḍit named Mām-hi-ka-wi and it is aifficult to restore this name into Sanskrit. The last two syllables are obscure. No grammarian from India posesses the name similar to this; but on the basis of the relation between the mentioned texts we may opine that *Mam-hi-ka-wi* is a corrupt form of the name *Mañjukrtī,* one of the proposed Sanskrit restorations for *jam-pai-grags-pa* name of the author of CH IV/6.

Refer CH IV/6 for detail.

According to the colophon the text on the technical derivations of *si* etc., which was composed by the great scholar *Mām-hi-ka-wi,* has been translated into Tibetan by the instructions of *blo-gros-brtaṅ-pa.* Again, it is known from the same source that all the necessary helps were given by *bla-ma chos-grags-dpal-bzaṅ-po* to complete this work; but the place of composition of the work is not mentioned any where in the treatise or in any other contemporary works. Some scholars opine that *blo-gros-rgyal-mtshan,* the translator of the work, was identical with the *sa-skya-pa* scholar who is known as *sa-bzaṅ-ma-ti-pan-chen. sa-bzaṅ* is the name of a monastery and the word-mati-is the Sanskrit equivalent of the Tibetan word '*blo-gros*': 'mind' or 'intelligence'.

Blo-gros-rgyal-mtshan along with *blo-gros-dpal-bzaṅ-po* had translated two works and our present treatise is one of them.65 Besides, a tantric work in the Peking bstan-'gyur is also attributed to these two translators. The former was an expert on Sanskrit grammar, who prepared an extension sub-commentary on the *Kātantra* grammar and the work is included in the *sa-skya—pai-bka'-bum.* The later, who was the co-translator, is also mentioned as the copyist of part of the work mentioned earlier i.e. CH IV/5 and was belonging to 14th century A.D. He was a disciple of *dpaṅ blo-gros-brtan-pa* (1st half of 14th century) and *dol-po-pa* (14th century A.D.) and worked on a revision of the translation of the *Kālacakratantra.*

Both of the translators were belonged to 14th century A.D. and on the basis of the date of the translators we may opine that the work was completed in 14th century A.D., but neither the present work nor the contemporary works mention the exact date of the translation.

CH IV/10: Title: *ka-lā-pa'i-byiṅs-kyi-mdo*
"Sūtras on verbal-roots of Kalāpa system".
[Pek. 5885, Nā. 3877, De. 4422]
Skt.: Title: Kalāpa-dhātu-sūtras
Author: Not mentioned
Translator/s: *'jam-dbyaṅs-ral-gri*
byaṅ-chub-rtse-mo and *'jam-dbyaṅs-ral-gri* (De.)
Place: *dpal (e'i-chos-gra)*
Date: 14th century A.D.

The work deals with the verbal roots associated to the *Kalāpa* system of Sanskrit grammar and the work seems to be closely related to the grammar prescribed by Pāṇini. Thieme (1932)[66] and Palsule (1961)[67] opine that this work on *dhātupāṭha* cannot be associated to the Kalāpa system and it seems to be a somewhat hapazard reworking of the Pāṇinian *dhātupāṭha* that came to be associated with the Kalāpa system. However, Liebich (1930: 216-232) considers it as the *dhātupāṭha* of the *Kātantra* and attributed it to Śarvavarman.

It is mentioned earlier in CH IV/7 that Durgasimha is the compiler of the *dhātupāṭha* literature in general. Here, neither the translator nor any contemporary work mentions the name of the author of the original Sanskrit work of the treatise. Again, the previous work bears a general title as: *Dhātu-kāya* and the title of the present treatise shows that this work is affiliated to the *Kalāpa* system only. A close study of these two treatises suggest that the work *Dhātukāya* is based on the *Cāndra* redaction and was adopted by the *Kalāpa* system also. (Refer CH IV/7 for detail). Thus, the work was more closely associated to the Kalāpa system. Now we may infer that this work was compiled by a sound scholar on the basis of the work of Durgasimha.

According to the colophon the work has been translated into Tibetan at the monastery of E', by *jam-dbyaṅs-ral-gri,* a great scholar on Sanskrit grammar and epistemology with the grace of his teacher *byaṅ-chub-rtse-mo* (14th century A.D.). Nothing more is available about the personal life and history of the translator; but he was flourished during the last quarter of 14th century A.D. and the work must have been translated during this time.[69]

For the place of translation refer CH IV/5.

CH IV/11: Title: *byiṅs-kyi-mdo*
"Sūtras on verbal-roots".
[Pek. 5887, Nā. 3879 De. 4424]
Skt.: Dhātu-sūtra
Author: Purṇacandra
Translator/s: *byaṅ-chub-rtse-mo*
blo-gros-brtan-pa and *byaṅ-chub-rtse-mo* (De.)
Place: Not mentioned
Date: 14th century A.D.

This is a treatise on the *Uṇādi sūtras* of the Kalāpa system of grammar with four *pādas.* These sūtras are the later additions to the *Kalāpa* system. These are attributed to Durgasimha, who is definitely later than Candragomin (5th century A.D.?) and probably flourished during 7th century A.D.

At the beginning of the treatise, the author salutes to Śiva for the happy ending of the work.[70] Since Durgasimha was a devotee of Lord Śiva we may argue that he was Hindu by religion and particularly a Saiva. In the Tibetan translations the opening of verse are meant for the goddess of speech, but not to Śiva.[71] According to the commentary in the opening verse speech has been personified as Sarasvatī. Here we may opine that the translator being Buddhist, salutes to the goddess Sarasvatī, but not to Śiva. It is also to mark that in the both translations i..e in this treatise and in the immediately following work, the homage verse is preceded by the homage to Manjuśrī, the Mahābodhisattva associated with speech.

Refer CH VII/5 for translator and CH IV/5 for the location of the place of translation.

CH IV/12: Title: *uṇ-la-sogs-pa'i-grel-pa*
"Commentary on *uṇ* and others.
Skt.: *Uṇādivṛtti.*

Author: Durgasimha
Translator/s: *rdo-rje-rgyal-mtshan*
Supervision: Śrīmāṇika and *dpal-ldan bsod-nams-bzaṅ-po.*
Place: *śel-dkar*
Date: 13th century A.D.

This is a commentary on the preceding *Uṇādi sūtra* text belonging to the *Kalāpa* system of Sanskrit grammar. Durgasimha (7th century A.D.) who is the author of the Uṇādi sūtras of the system is also the author of the commentary. Thus, we may say that this is an auto-commentary by the author of the sūtras. Here the author describes the derivational procedure involved in the application of the Uṇādi suffixes in question, quoting sūtras from the text and examples especially from the *dhātupāṭha* as is common in commentaries on Uṇādi sūtras.

Like the previous work this has four sections (pāda) in total.[73] Though the translation of the *Uṇādi* sūtras as incorporated in this work varies slightly from that of CH IV/11, the redactions of the original sūtra text in either treatise correspond closely.

Refer CH IV/8 for translator.

Śrīmāṇika,[74] the supervisor of the translator, supervised the translaion done by our translator i.e. CH IV/8 and 12. Like Śrīmāṇika, *bsod-nams-bzaṅ-po* (13th century) also supervised the translator for his two translations.

CH IV/13: Title: *ti-la-sogs-pa'i-mtha'i-bya-ba'i-tshing-gsal-ba.*
"Derivation of the forms ending in 'ti' etc."
[Pek. 5897, Nā. 3889, De. 4452].
Skt.: *Tyādyantasya prakriyā-pada-rohaṇa*
Author: *dga'-ba'i-grags-pa*
Translator/s: Dharmaśrībhadra
Place: *ri-phug*
Date: 14th century A.D.

This work belongs to the *Kātantra* system of Sanskrit grammar. It begins with a short synopsis of the nominal casendings. The title of the work suggests that this is a work on verbal conjugations. The whole text consists of sixteen sections, of which only the first ten are explicitly numbered. The first ten deal with the ten tenses and moods viz. present indicative,[75] optative,[76] imperative,[77] imprefect,[78] aorist,[79] perfect,[80] periphrastic future,[81] precative,[82] simple future[83] and conditional.[84] However, the first section is divided into ten sub-sections, dealing with the ten classes of verbs.[85] It is to mark that the traditional third class of roots is incorporated within the second class in this work which is a typical style of the *Kātantra* classification of the verbal bases (CH IV/7-8 and 10). Section eleven to sixteen of this treatise deal with desideratives, medial intensives, active intensives, causatives, causative-desideratives and denominatives.[86]

The author of this work is *dga'-ba'i-grags-pa* and the name may be reconstructed in Sanskrit as Nandakīrti. However, this name is not popular in the Indian grammatical traditions. However, such a name is mentioned in the bibliography of the "encyclopedia of Indian philosophies [The Philosophy of the grammarians, Vol. V p. 527, M.L.B.D. 1990].[87] But, some scholars suggests that the name of the author of this work (Sanskrit) was Utsavakīrti.

No sanskrit ms. of the treatise is available now. However, Sāṅkṛtyāyana's "Sanskrit palm-leaf manuscripts' contains a 123-leaf ms. entitled *Kalāpavyākaraṇa-tikā* which was preserved in the *ṅor e-wam-chos-sde* monastery in central Tibet. The author of this ms. was Utsavakrīt.[88] We may identify Utsavakīrti with the Tibetan name *dga'-ba'i-grags-pa*, as both the names can be translated as 'having fame of joy'. Again the New Catalogues Catalogorum[89] suggests that Utsavakīrti was the author of the *Pdasūryaprakriyā*, a work on the *Kātantra* system of Sanskrit grammar. However, the colophon of the work entitled *Tyādy-antasya prakriyā-pada rohanam-nāma* refers to an Indian ms., a hand book of *spyal-lo-tstsha-ba*, which was used for this translation. Some scholars dare to suggest that the ms. which was kept at *Ṅor* monastery was used as the basic text for the translation of the work under discussion.

Dharmaśrībhadra, the translator of this text, was possibly an Indian-Buddhist monk. Since he is mentioned along with *Bu-ston rin-chen-grub* (1st half of 14th century A.D.), he may not be confused with his namesakes from the eighth century[90] and the tenth-eleventh century.[91] He was a spiritual son of *bu-ston rin-chon-grub*, specialized in Sanskrit linguistics but also proficient in logic and *tantra*. He became a zha-lu-dge-bśes and resided in the *ri-phug* hermitage, which is allied to *zha-lu* monastery.[92]

Ri-phug is an important religions centre, which is founded by Dipamkaraśrījñāna (982 A.D. to 1054 A.D.), the famous Indian Paṇḍit viz.,*paṇḍta-di-pam-ka-ra-śrī-dznā-na'i-byin-gyis-brlabs-pa'i-chos-gnas-chen-po-ri-phug.*

This location may be identified as the *ri-phug* hermitage in the mountains to the north-east of *zha-lu,* in *gtsaṅ* province. Sāṅkṛtyā-yana (1937) suggests that it is a monastery near the *zha-lu* monastery.

Notes and References

1. Cf.; ... *tena tantramiha sūtramucyate /iṣat tantram kātantram /ku śabdasya tantra śabde pare ka tviśadarthejñaḥ (S.II /5 /25) itisadarthe kādeśaḥ /*
   The Katantrapañjikā of Trilocanadāsa; p. 466.
2. Cf; *kālena sarvavarmākhyo mantr saha maya nṛpam /provāca rajannasthane ko'yan sokagrahastava //*
   The Bṛhatkathāmañjarī I-3-42.
3. Refer The Bṛhatkathāmañjarī, III/IV.
4. Dash, N.K., The Kalāpa system of Sanskrit grammar (unpublished).
5. Belvalkar, S.K., Systems of Sanskrit grammar, pp. 68-76.
6. Dash, N.K.; The Kalāpa system of Sanskrit grammar (unpublished).
7. Cf; *sarba-wa-rma,* Chandra, L; (ed), 1965-71, Vol. 24; 864-2.
8. Cf; *sapta-wa-rma;* Tāranāha:—Schiefner, A; (ed); Tāranātha de doctrinae buddhicae in India propagatione narratio, Petropolis, 1968, p. 60 and koṅ-sprul:— Chandra, L. (ed.) 1970, Vol. 1: 35.1.
9. Refer, Schiefner, A; Tāranātha's Geschichte des Buddhismus in India, St. Petrsburg, 1869, p. 76.
10. dbaṇ-phyug-go-cha, Schiefner, A (ed.); 1868, p. 60.
11. Refer, Cordier, P; Catalogue du Fonds tibéetain de la Bibliotheque Nationale 3e partie: Index du Bstan-'gyur, Paris 1915, pp. 460-461.
12. Refer; the Kathāsaritsāgara, VI/108-164.
13. Refer; the Bṛhatkathāmañjarī, VI/35-52.
14. Refer, Chandra, L (Ed.), 1965-1971, Vol. 24: 864.3-4.

15. Cf; *snar-bod-du-grags-pa;'i-lo-rgyus-ltar-na-ka-lā-pa'i-kun-bśad-bzhi-pa-yan-chad-gzhon-nu-gdoṅ-drug-gis-bśad-cin-|;* Schiefner, A., 1868, p. 60.
16. The enumeration of Sanskrit phonemes, differently ordered than the traditional alphabet, which serves as basis for the so-called *pratyāhāra-sūtras* i.e. abbreviated forms indicating groups of phonemes, on the *Śiva-sūtras* and their function please refer Cardona, G; 1976, pp.209-10.
17. Refer: Kā I-1-1 to 12 especially-*siddho varṇa-samāmnāyaḥ* I-1-1.
18. This notion of morphophonemic change, similarly expressed, is ready to be found in the *Prātiśākhyas,* the Linguistic branches of the Vedic Literature.
19. Cf; *tshul-'di-dpal-sa-skya-ru /*
blo-gros-brtan-pa-gsum-pa-yis /
dur-ga-siṅ-ha'i-'grel-pa-la /
brten-nas-sgra-don-ji-bzhin-bsgyur /
[Pek. 110 r2-3]
20. Refer; Lalou, M; Repertoire du Tanjur d'apres le catalogue de P. cordir, avec une preface de paul pelliot, Paris, 1933, p. 200.
21. Refer; Ferrari, A; Mk'yen brtse's Guide to the Holy Places of Central Tibet, Roma, 1958, pp. 63-64 and 148-151.
22. Cf; Sāṅkṛtyāyana, R; Sanskrit palm-leaf mss. in Tibet, JBORS XXI, 1, 1935, pp. 21-43.
23. A second translation of the text is also found in the Bstan-'gyur which was translated by Dpal-ldan Blo-gros-brtan-pa (Pek. 125v3) at the noble monastery Gnas-po-che (Pek. 125V4). It is also known from the colophon of the work that the translator had translated the work only after a comparison of the work with the Pañjikā of Trilocanadāsa (cf; Pek. 125V3-5). However this second translation contains some more of the text.
24. Refer the colophon of this work which was translated by *blo-gros-brtan-pa* viz., *zhes-pa-durga-siṅhis-mdzad-pa'i-'grel-par-miṅ-bzhi-par-rkaṅ-daṅ-po-rdzogs-so //*[Pek. 125V3]
25. Refer the note no. 23 above.
26. Cf; Sāṅkṛtyāyana, R; Second Search of Sanskrit Palm-leaf Mss. in Tibet, JBORS, XXIII, 1, 1937, pp. 1-57.
27. Cf; Abhyankar, K.V; 1977, pp. 76-77; and Belvalkar, S.K.; 1915, p.91.
28. Cf; *dpal-ldan-tiṅ-'dzin-bzaṅ-po'i-zhabs /*
bsñen-pa'i-sgrol'ba'i-dbaṅ-phyug-gis /
slob-ma-la-phan-rgya-mtsho-las /
/grel-pa-ñuṅ-ṅu-'di-btus-byas /... etc.
[Pek. 163v3-4; Co. 62v3-4]

29. Refer the colophon Pek. 163v2-5 and Co. 62V3-4 for details viz., *lha-bla-ma-zhi-ba-'od-kyis-zhaṅ-zhuṅ-gi-sa-cha /tho-liṅ-gser-gyi-gtsug-lag-khaṅ-du-bsgyur-ba'o //* It means: Royal Lama *Zhi-a-'od* has translated the text in the *gser-gyi-gtsug-lag-khaṅ* (Golden Temple) of *Tho-liṅ.* in the country of *Zhaṅ-zhuṅ.*
30. Refer the note 29 above.
31. Cf; Co-ne *dkar-chag* 294v1-2. *luṅ-du-ston-pa-ka-lā-pa'i-'grel-ba-paṇḍita-bgrod-dka'-seṅ-ges-mdzad-pa /bu-ston-lo-tsā-ba'i-'gyur /*
32. Cf; CH IV/4, CH III/9 and CH IV/7.
33. Refer, Ruegg. D.S.; The life of Bu ston rin po che, with the Tibetan text of the Buston rnam thar, Roma, 1966, p. 81; 11a4-11a7.
34. Cf; *de-bar-la-sgra-ka-lā-pa'i-'grel-pa-durga-siṅha'i-'phro-bsgyur* /Ibid, 1966, p. 122: 23ab-2317.
35. Refer, Belvalkar, S.K.; 1915, p.91 and Abhyankar, K.V.; 1977, pp. 76-77.
36. Cf; CH IV/1.
37. Cf; Belvalkaar, S.K., 1915, pp. 83-85 and 91.
38. Ibid, p. 85.
39. The full title of the lexicon is: *legs-par-sbyar-ba-lha'i-skad-daṅ-gaṅs-can-pa'i-brda'-śan-sbyar-ba-dri-bral-nor-bu'i-me-loṅ;* completed in 1771. One of its many sections deals with the technical terms occuring in the sub-section on feminine suffixes in Ugrabhuti's Kalāpa commentary. The title of the section is: *ka-lā-pa'i-gzhuṅ-gi-kha-skoṅ-jo-bo-drag-'byor-gyis-sbyor-ba'i-miṅ-le-bdun-pa-bud-med-kyi-rkyen-mtha.*
40. Cf; *sñoms-ehuṅ [sic] -lo-tstsha-ba-dpal-ldaṇ-blo-gros-brtan-pas-bsgyur-bai'i-yi-ge-pa-ni-sde-snod-'dzin-pa-chen-po-rig-pa'i-rgyal-po-zhes-bya-ba'o* /[Pek. 28v4]
41. Refer Pek. 51V* to 52r3.
42. Cf; *e-chos-'byuṅ-gi-gtsug-lag-khaṅ-du-skad-gñis-pa-deg-sloṅ-byaṅ-chub-rtse-mos-bsgyur-ba'o //* [Pek. 86v1-2]
43. Cf; Pek. 214v4.
44. Cf; *dpaṅ-lotstsha-ba-dpal-ldan-blo-gros-brtan-pas-bsgyur-ba'o* / [Pek. 232v6}
45. Cf; Pek. 295v-7 and Co. 319r6-7.
46. Cf; *dbyaṅs-mtha'-can-rnams-skyes-pa-la- ...* /
[Pek. 164v2-172r8] for 1.1.
Also *gsal-byed-kyi-mtha'-can ...*
[Pek. 172r8-179v2] for 1.2.
Also
bud-med-kyi-dbyaṅs-kyi-mtha'-can-rnams

[Pek. 183v5-190r8] for 3.1.
Also Pek. 190r8 to 193v1 for 3.2.

47. Refer Pek. 193v1 to 229r2 for detail.
48. Refer Pek. 179v2-189v5.

Now we would like to give a list of the words those are dealt with in this text. In 1.1 we have the following word: *vipra, hāhā, agni, sakhi, pati, vāta-pramī, amśu, kroṣṭu, pratibhū, nagnaku, pitṛ, nṛ, praśastṛ, rai, go and glau* /Pek. 164v2-172r8 /. In 1.2 we have the following stems: *kamuc, bhubhuj, saṃrāj, matut (marut), udanvat, kravyad, mṛgābadh, ātman, rājan, yuvan, śvan, maghavan, arvan, panthān, puṣan, brahmahan, śasin, viś, dviṣ, vedhas, uśan, purudamś, anhas, pums, anadvaḥ, madhulih, mtradruḥ and kāṣṭhatakṣ [Peek. 172v1-179v1] Inthe chapter Two the following stems are dealt with: vana, vāri, asthi, vastu, aśri, viyat, sāman, ahen, ḳarman, vār, sarpis, vapus* and *utas* [Pek. 179v3-183v2]

Stems dealt with in 3.1: *jāyā, jarā, niśā, bhūmi, nadī lakṣmī, śrī, nī, strī, dhenu, vadhu, bhrū, punarbhū, mātṛ, svasṛ, se, dyo and nau* [Pek. 183v8-190r8].

Stms dealt with in 3.2: *vāc, sraj, yoṣit, śarad, kṣudh, pāman, ap, kukubh, gir, dvar, div, diś, prabhṛṣ, sumanas, bhās, āśis, uṣṇih, snuh* and *upānaḥ* [Pek. 190v1-193r8]

4.1: *śukla, kilālapā, śūci, grāmaṇī, sudhī, paṭu citragu śikharalū, subhrū, kartṛ, sumātṛ, arcite, bahura, atidyo* and *sunau* [Pek. 193v3-199r3]

4.2: *Kāṣṭhaśak, citralikh, aṅgalag, bahuślagh, paṭhitaliṅ, vyaktavāc, prāñc, pratyañe, udañc, adamuyañc sadhryañc, samyañc, tiryañc, mulavṛkc, śabdaprāch, yuj aśvayuj, dhānābhṛj, sthānamasj, likhitajh, janojjh, paṭhitañ, bhikṣaṭ, sāmapaṭh, sūtratuḍ, likhitaDh, sugaṇ agnicit, āyusmat, kiyat, iyat, etāvat, mahat, bṛhat bhavat, [words ending in-at] agnimath, kāṣṭhabhid, gaganarudh, tatvabudh, dhanin, pīvan, paralokadṛśan maṇḍapalip, bahvap, svap, arituph, kṣīb, kṛtānuṣṭubh, praśam, mañjugir, paṭhitaha, vimaladiv, dṛṣṭadiś, dalaspṛś, mūladaś, ratnamus, dadhṛs, grāmaṇis, kaṭacikrs, māmsapipakṣ, tasthivams, śreyas, ukhāsras, anupānaḥ, grāmadah, pṛṣṭhavḥ,* and *gorakṣ* {Pek. 199r7-213r7]

4.3 *sarvaka, viśva, ubhaka, ubhayaka, anyaka, tvaka, tvat / tvakat, nemaka, pūrva etc., tyad, tyakad, tad / takad, yad / yakad, adas / adakas, idam / idakam, ena, etad / etakad, ena, eka, kim, dvika, yuṣmad, asmad* and *bhavat* [Pek. 213v3-226r3]

4.4 *eka, tri, catur, pañcan, ṣaṣ, saptan, aṣṭan, and remaining numreals with kati* and *yati.*

49. Refer, Sāṅkṛtyāyana, R; 1930, p. 40, Ms. no. 153.
50. Cf; /*rnam-par-gnon-pa'i-ṅaṅ-tshul-padma'i-'byuṅ-gnas-kyi[Co. kyis] /*
/*ṅaṅ-ba'i-rgyal-pa-sgra-yi-rgya-mstho'i-skye-ba-'dzin /*
/*mkhas-pa-dpal-ldan-'jam-pa'i-grags-pas*[Pek. phas]-byas-par-gyur // [Pek. 299r3-4 and Co. 54r6-7]
51. According to the colophon our translator had translated the text in the monastic academy of *gnas-po-che* viz., *lo-tsā* [Pek. tsa] —*ba'i-miṅ-tsam-'dzin-pa-sñoms-las-pa / dge-sloṅ-dpal-ldan-blo-gros-brtan-pas / /dpal-gnas-po-che'i-gtsug-lag-khaṅ-du-bsgyur-ba'o* //[Pk. 2294r; Co. 54r7].
52. Cf; *bgrod-dka'-seṅ-ges-sbyar-ba-yi / dgu-yi-graṅs-kyi-byiṅs-kyi-gzhuṅ /de-ni-sum-cu-rtsa-lṅa-yis /lhag-pa'i-sum-brgyur-śes-par-bya / byiṅs-kyi-tshogs-rdzogs-so /* [Pek. 435r5, Co. 74v6-7].
53. Cf; Palsule, G.B; The Sanskrit *Dhātupāṭhas*—A critical study, Poona, 1961, p. 51.
54. *Kaiścic curādiṣu yujādayaḥ paṭhyante* (Palsule 1961, p. 52) - *kha-cig-tu-tsu-ra-la-sogs-pa-rnams-su-ya (yu)-dza-la-sogs-pa-rnams-klog-par-byed-de* [Pek. 434v4]5].
55. It is also to mark that the beginning section is divided into 10 sub-sections *ad* etc. hu ek *div* etc., *su* etc. *tu* etc., *rudh* etc., *tan* etc., *kṛ* etc., *cur* etc. and the last sub-sction is incorporated with presnt *ātmanepada* forms in denotations ***bhāva*** and ***karman*** i.e. passive conjugation [Pek. 207v3-248r2].
The second section deals with 'optative', that third dals with 'imperative', the fourth deals with 'imprfect', the fifth deals with 'arorist', the sixth deals with 'perfect', the seventh deals with 'periphrastic future', the eight deals with 'precative', the ninth deals with 'future and the tenth section deals with 'conditional' rules. [Pek. 248r2 to 319v4].
56. Section 11: *san'i-mtha'-mdor-bstan-pa* 'desideratives'.
Section 12: *yin'i-mtha'-mdor-bstan-pa-*'denominatives'
Section 13: *kā-mya'i-mtha'-mdor-bstan-pa* 'denominatives ending in kāmya'
Section 14: *ñe-bar-'jal-ba-las-yin-mdor-bstan-pa* 'denominatives denoting comparison'
Section 15: *ā-yi-la-sogs-pa* 'denominatives in āya'.
Section 16: *in-mtha'-las-san-mdor-bstan-pa* 'causatives and their derivations'.
Section 17: *tse-krī-yi-ta-mdor-bstan-pa* 'intensives (medium)'.
Section 18: *tṣe-krī-yi-ta-zhig-pa'i-mtha'i-mdor-bstan-pa* 'intensives with elision of vikaraṇa'.

Section 19: *yin'i-mtha'-las-san'o* 'desideratives derived from denominatives'.

57. Refer note 55 above.
58. The technical terms and the ordering used for the various tenses and moods are like the following:
vartamāna [Pek. 207v3, Kā. III] 1/11/; *saptami*
[Pek. 248 r2, Kā, III/1/20]; *pañcamī*
[Pek. 251 v7, Kā. III/1/18]; *hyastanī*
[Pek. 258 r2, Kā. III/23]; *adyatani*
[Pek. 264 r5, Kā. III/22]; *parokṣā*
[Pek. 284 v8, Kā. III/1/13]; *śvastanī*
[Pek. 302 v7, Kā, III/1/15]; *āśis*
[Pek. 308 v8, Kā. III/1/15]; *bhaviṣyanti*
[Pek. 314 r5, Kā. III/1/15] and *kriyātipatti*
These technical terms are used in the sense of 'present indicative', 'optative', 'imperative', 'imperfect', 'aorist', 'parokṣā', 'periphrastic future', 'precative', and 'conditional' respectively.
59. Rahula Sāṅkṛtyāyana lists a ms. entitled Ty-ādy-anta-prakriyā of Sarvadhara in *māgadhi* which was kept in the Ṅor E-wam-chos-sde monastry in Central Tibet [1936, p. 36, sl. No. 164].
60. Ibid.
61. Cf; Cordier III, P. 468. JASB. 1907, p. 131, JBORS, XXI, i. 36; vide New Catalogus Catalogorum, Vol. 8, 1974, Madras Univrsity, p. 227.
62. Ibid.
63. Refer Pek. 365 r6-6 and Co. 236 v7-337 r4 for the colophon.
64. The declanations of the followign words have been dealt with in the chapters of the text:
1.1: *sūrya, agni, sakhi, pati, pathi, amśu, kroṣṭu svayambhū, pitṛ, nṛ, praśastṛ, rai, go* and *glau* (masculine ending in vowel, Tib. skyes-pa'i-rtags-dbyaṅs-kyi-mtha'-can-rnams).
1.2: *ambumuc, kṣmā-bhuj, marut, kravyād, mṛgavyadh, ātman, rājan, yugan, śvan, maghavan, pūṣan, brahmahan halin, viś, dviś, vedhas, uśanas, anehas, dos, pums, anaḍvah, madhulih, vimuh, mitraduh, kāṣṭhatakṣ* (masculine ending in consonant, Tib. gsal-byed-kyi-mtha'-can-mams).
2.1: *uana, vāri, asthi* and *vastu* (neuter ending in vowel, Tib. *ma-min-gi-rtags-dbyaṅs-kyi-mtha'-can-rnams).*
2.2: *jagat, dāman, ahan, karman, sarpis, vapus* and *tejas* (neuter ending in consonant, Tib. ma-niṅ-gi-rtags-gsal-byed-kyi-mtha'-can-rnams).
3.1: *jāyā, jarā, nadī, lakṣmī, śrī, strī, bhūmi, vadhū, bhrū punarbbū, dhenu, svasṛ* and *mātṛ* (feminine ending in vowel,

Tib. bud-med-kyi-rtags-can-rnams).

3.2: *vāc, sraj, vidyut, dṛśad, krudh, dāman, ap, kakubh, gir, dhur, dvār, vār, div, dis, pravis, sumanas, bhās, āśis uṣṇih* and *upānah* (femnine ending in consonant).

4.1: *śukla, kilālapā, śuci, grāmaṇī, sudhī, paṭu, kamalū, kartṛ, sumātṛ, bahurai, sunau* and *citragu* (adjectives ending in vowel, Tib. thun-moṅ-brjod-par-byed-pa'i-dbyaṅs-mtha'-can).

4.2: *sa. javāc, aśvayuj, ardhabhaj, śabdaprāṣ, pathiprach, devej, dhānābhṛjj, mulavṛkh, prāñc, pratyañc, go-añc, udañc, viśvañc, adamuyañc, sadhryañc, samyañc, tiryañc, sukruñc, sugan, āyuṣmat, kṛtavat, yuvan, kiyat, mahat, bṛhat, bhavat, etc., śakruñjit, takramath, durghapad, tattvavid, jñānabudh, dhanin, pīvān, arvan, paralokadṛś, kṛtānuṣṭubh, praśam, vimaladiv, dṛṣṭadiś, tāṛś, svarṇamuṣ dadhṛṣ, testhivams, vidvams, prajiyas, śreyas,* various comparativs in iyas and superlatives in *iṣṭha, ukhāsras, praṣṭauh, goduh* and *svanadvaḥ* (adjectives ending in consonants, Tib. thun-moṅ-brjod-par-byed-pa'i-rtags-gsal-byed-kyi-mtha'-can-rnams).

5.1: *sarva, viśva, ubha, ubhaya, anya, anyatara, itara, Datara, pṛta, tva, nema, soma, sima, pūrva, para, adas, idam etad, kim, eka, dvi, yuṣmad, asmad* and *bhavat* (prnouns, Tib. sorba'i-miṅ-ca-rnams).

6.1: *tri (priyatri), catur (priyacatur), kati, pañcan, ṣaṣ (priyaṣaṣ), saptan, aṣṭan, navan, daśan* and numerals (main) from 20 upwards (numrals three and higher, Tib. graṅs-kyi-sgra-las-gsum-la-sogs-pa).

65. Cf; the Colophon: *zhes-pa-mkhas-pa'i-dbaṅ-po-dpal-blo-gros-brtan-pa'i-legs-par-bśad-pa-daṅ /bla-ma-dam-pa-chos-grags-dpal-bzaṅ-po'i-bka'-luṅ-daṅ /mthun-rkyen-phun-sum-tshogs-pa-la-brten-nas-sgra-rig-pa'i-dge-sloṅ-lo-tsā-ba-blo-gros-rgyal-mtshan-daṅ /blo-gros-dpal-bzaṅ-pos-legs-par-bsgyur-ciṅ-zhus-te-gtan-la-phab-pa'o //* [Co. 98rb].

66. Thieme, P; zur Geschichte der einheimishcen Indischen Grammatik', Orientalische Literatur zeitung, 4, 1932, pp. 239-40.

67. Palsule, G.B. The Sanskrit Dhātupāṭhas—A cirtical study, Poona, 1961, pp. 36-41.

68. The colophon suggest that this work belongs to the *Kalāpa* system: *ces-pa-kā-la-pa'i-byiṅs-kyi-mdo-rdzogs-so //* [Pek. 304r3].

69. Refer the Colophon: *byiṅs-kyi-glegs-bam-dgos-'dod-'byuṅ-ba-'di /*

paṇ-chen-byaṅ-chub-rtse-mo'i-bka'-drin-las /sgra-daṅ-tshad-ma'i-de-ñid-rg-pa-can /'jam-dbyaṅs-ral-gri-zhes-byas-legs-par-

sgyur . dpal-e'i-chos-grar-sgyur-ba'o /
[Pek. 304 r3-4]

70. *namaskṛtya śivam bhūriśabdasantānakāriṇam* /
uṇādayo vidhsyante bālavyutpattihetave //
Refer Belvalkar, 1915, p. 88.

71. Cf; /*rgyud-kyi-sgra-ni-maṅ-po'i-rgya* /
/*ṅag-las-rab-tu-phyag-'tshal-te* /
/*byis-pas-rab-tu-rtogs-phyir-du* /
/*uṇ-la-sogs-nas-bsgrub-par-bya* //
[Pek. 323 r2-3]
Besides, in the commentary of this text (CH IV/12) we have the introductory verse as:
sa-steṅ-sgra-yi-rgyud-rnams-ni /
/*byed-pa'i-ṅag-la-phyag-byas-te* /
/*byis-pa-bye-brag-rtogs-pa'i-rgyur* /
/*uṇ-la-sogs-rnams-sgrub-byed-'gyur* /
[Pek. 326 r2].

72. Cf; e.g. Liebich (1902: IX) who used the *Cāndra uṇādi-vṛtti* as one of the sources for his edition of the *Cāndra dhātupāṭha*, Cf; also CH III/13 and CH III/16.
73. Refer Pek. 326r1 to 365r2.
74. Lalou reads the name as Māṇika only. Cf; Lalou, M; Repertoire du Tanjur d'apresle Catalogue de P. Cordier, avec une Preface de Paul Pelliot, Paris, 1933, p. 158.
75. Cf; *daṅ-po-bartta-mā-nā'i-yul-la-bstan-pa* / [Pek. 3v5-36v3].
76. Cf; *gñis-pa-sapta—mī'i-yul-bstan-pa* [Pek. 36v3-37v4].
77. *-gsum-pa-pañtsa-mī'i-yul-bstan-pa-* /[Pek. 37v4-40r8].
78. *-bzhi-pa-hya-sta-nī'i-yul-bstan-pa-* /[Pek. 40r8-43r3].
79. *-lṅa-pa-a-dya-ta-nī'i-yul-bstan-pa-* /[Pek. 43r3-50r6].
80. *-drug-pa-pa-ro-kṣa'i-yul-bstan-pa-* /[50r6-57r6].
81. *-bdun-pa-śva-sta-nī'i-yul-mdor-bstan-pa-* / [Pek. 57r6-60v4].
82. *-brgyad-pa-ā-śiśi-yul-bstan-pa-* /[Pek. 60v4-61v3].
83. *-dgu-pa-bha-bi-syantī'i-yul-mdor-bstan-pa-* /[Pek. 61v3-62v1].
84. *-bcu-pa-kṛ-ya-ti-pattī'i-yul-mdor-bstan-pa-* /[Pek. 62v1-5].
85. These sub-seitons deal with the gaṇas from bhvādi to *curādi*. / Pek. 3v5-36v3/.
86. Refer Pek. 62v5-78r6.
87. Here, the editors follow the New Cat. Cat. vol. 8. p. 159.
88. Sāṅkṛtāyana, R; 1935, no. 152, p. 40.
89. Cf; "Utsavakīrti, surnamed Sāraṅga Upādhyāya. Padasūryaprakriyā (-vyākaraṇa). Aindra or Kātantra school of grammar." New Catalogue Catalogorum, Vol. 2., University

of Madras, 1966, p. 322. Also refer New Cat. Cat. vol./III, p. 309 (B) and vol. XI, P. 103.

90. Refer, Lalou, M; 1933, p. 150: "contemporary de Jñānakumāra".
91. Refer, Ibid; "contemporary de Śraddhākaravarman".
92. Refer; Khetsun Sangpo; Biographical Dictionary of Tibet and Tibetan Buddhism (in 11 vols.), vol. XI Dharmasala, 1973-1980, pp. 82-84.

5

SĀRASVATA SYSTEM OF SANSKRIT GRAMMAR

History of Sārasvata grammar (Indian tradition) :

The original Sārasvata-sūtras are attributed to the name Narendrācārya.[1] He is said to have composed around 700 mūla-sūtras under the inspiration of Sarasvatī. The calculation of the sūtras (i.e. little less than 700) is based on a Ms. which has been preserved in the Deccan College (No. 239 of 1892-95). This Ms. has 597 mūlasūtras plus 91 more vārttikas. Thus, the total number of the *sūtras* seem to be (597 + 91) = 688. Belvalkar suggests that the original order of the sūtras seem to be preserved in this Ms. only and all other MSS. usually follow the order of Anubhūtisvarūpācārya's Sārasvata-prakriyā.[2]

The Sārasvata school appears to have been popular in northern India from its inception in 13th century down to the time of Bhaṭṭoji Dīksita (17th century), when the revival of the Pāṇinian tradition put most of the other schools of grammar into a decline.

In 1270 A.D.[3] Anubhutisvarūpācārya rearranged[4] the whole Sārasvata-mūla-sūtras and added some *Vārttika* and *sūtras* for the logical presentation of the work. this work of Anubhutisvarūpācārya is called Sārasvata-prakriyā.

This Sārasvata-prakriyā was short and to the point and therefore, it was an easy method to learn Sanskrit grammar. Gradually it became popular and a good number of commentators composed their own commentaries on this in between 15th century A.D. to 18th century A.D.

History of Sārasvata grammar (Tibetan tradition)

According to the Tibetan source (Bu-ston and Tāranātha are silent about this system) the author of this system is Anubhuti, a Maharastrian Brahmin.[5] His text book is considered to have been revealed to him by the goddess *Sarasvatī* (Tib. dbyaṅs-can).[6] Koṅ-sprul also opines that the author Anubhutisvarūpācārya wrote an auto-commentary on his grammatical sūtras, entitled Prakriyā-caturā (Tib. rab-byed-gsal-ldan)[7] or *Sārasvataprakriyā*.[8] The Tibetan source further suggests that a great number of commentaries on the Sārasvata system were written in India. However, Koṅ-sprul mentions only one author of these commentaries, viz. Puñjarāja.[9] Belvalkar suggests that "he was a minister to Gaisudin Khilji of Malva (1469-1500)".[10] Abhyankar opines Puñjarāja was a "grammarian of the twelfth century".[11] Again Abhyankar identifies the Puñjarāja with Punyarāja, the commentator of the two *kāṇḍas* of the Vākyapadīya of Bhartṛhari. He however, categorically suggests that "a scholar called Puñjarāja, but different from above, is known to have written a commentary on the Sārasvataprakriyā.[12] But, Abhyankar has not given any more information regarding him. Some scholars wrongly assume that both the commentator of Sārasvataprakriyā i.e. Puñjarāja and the Punyarāja, the commentator of the Vākyapadīya are same and identical. While the later flourished during 12th century A.D., the former flourished during the later half of 15th Century A.D.

Koṅ-sprul, further, suggests that Tāranātha, the famous polymath of the *jo-naṅ-pa sect*, together with two Indian Paṇḍits, viz., Kṛṣṇa and Balabhadra, has done the translation of the basic sūtra-text (parcial) i.e. CH V/1. The colophon of the text (CH V/1), however, mentions both Tāranātha and Paṇḍit Kṛṣṇa (bhaṭṭa) as translators of the text.[13]

The same source states that the second translation of the Sārasvata root-text (i.e. CH V/2), was made by the translator from *'dar, Ṅag-dbaṅ-phun-tshogs-lhun-grub* (17th century A.D.). The colophon suggests that this translation was made in collaboration with two Indian Paṇḍits i.e. Balabhadra and Gokulanātha Mishra, who also worked for the translations of the works on Pāṇini's grammar.

The same three translators also produced a translation of the Prakriyā-caturā commentary (i.e. CH V/3) translation.

On the other hand he mentions a translation of Anubhūti's auto-commentary Prakriyā-caturā by *Chos-kyi-snaṅ-ba* with the assistance of a Nepal Brahmin called Viṣṇupati.[14] Since this translation has not been incorporated into the Buddhist canon it is not possible for us to trace the work and to make study on that. Further, Ko. mentions about the commentary of Tāranātha on Sārasvata-vyākaraṇa. So far no copy of this text has come to notice.

CH V/1

Title : *brda-sprod-pa-dbyaṅs-can / dbyaṅs-can-ma-brda-sprod-pa*

"Sarasvatī Grammar"

[Pek. 5886, Nā. 3878, De. 4423].

Skt : *Sarasvatīvyākaraṇa/Sārasvatavyākaraṇa*

Author : Anubhūtisvarūpācārya.

Translator/s : Kṛṣṇabhaṭṭa and Tāranātha

Place : Not mentioned

Date : 1st half of 17th century A.D.

This is the basic text of the Sārasvata system of Sanskrit grammar, consisting of sūtras and auto commentary on the sūtras. The sūtras and the commentary there on are attributed to Anubhutisvarūpācārya (about 1270 A.D.). This grammar appears to have been popular in northern India from its inception in 13th century down to the time of Bhaṭṭoji Dikṣita (17th century A.D.), when the revival of the Pāṇinian tradition put most of the other schools of grammar into a decline. In the present translation, however, the translator does not mention the name of the original author. The present translation is incomplete and bears only the first of the total of four sections. The first section has five sub-sections and these deal with the chapter called *samdhi* 'euphonic combination'. Beside the present work, we have another two Tibetan translations of this system of grammar (CH V/2 and-3); but while the treatise CH V/2 has only the translation of the sūtras, the other work is incorporated with the translation of the commentary. However, these two works are complete as these bear the whole text.

According to the colophon the work has been translated by two sound scholars named Kṛṣṇabhaṭṭa and Tāranātha; but the place of their work is not mentioned any where.[15]

Kṛṣṇabhaṭṭa was an Indian Paṇḍit (composed the Vākyacandrikā? N.C.C. IV/335) and flourished during the last quarter of 16th century A.D. or early parts of 17th century A.D. Nothing more about this scholar is known to us.

Tāranātha was a great polymath scholar and translator belonging to the Jo-naṅ-pa sect of Buddhism. Though he was a translator, still he was famous for his religious history.[16] In this treatise though the translator has not mentioned the date, still we might suppose it to have been made at a later date than Tāranātha's historiography. which he composed in 1608, as this system of grammar does not appear in his work of 1608 A.D.

It is known from the colophon that Tāranātha was assisted by Kṛṣṇabhaṭṭa for the translation of this text; but *Koṅ-sprul' śes-bya-kun-khyub* states that for this first translation of the Sārasvata sūtras, Tāranātha was not only assisted by Kṛṣṇabhaṭṭa, but also by Balabhadra, an Indian scholar.[17] Further it is known from the same source that the Tibetan scholar Tāranātha had composed a commentary on Sārasvata grammar.[18]

CH V/2 : Title : *brda-sprod-pa'i-dbyaṅs-can-gyi-mdo.*
"Sarasvatī Grammar's rules".
[Pek. 5911, Nā. 3903, De. 4297 and Co. SE 1]
Skt : Sarasvatī-vyākaraṇa-sūtra
Author : Anubhūtisvarūpācārya?
Translator/s : *dar Ṅag-dbaṅ-phun-tshogs-lhun-grub* and Gokula Misra
[Tā. Balabhadra]
Place : Potala
Date : 17th Century A.D.

This is a basic sūtra text of the Sārasvata system with four broad sections, dealing with *Samdhi* "euphonic combination", nouns, verbs and primary nominal suffixes.[19] The *samdhi* section is incorporated with five sub-section : introduction to technical terms, *samdhi* of vowels, hiatus (*pragṛhya*), *samdhi* of consonants and of *visarga*. The second section has twelve sūtra sections: declension of masculine, feminine and neuter stems ending in vowels and in consonants, feminine forming suffixes; case-semantics, nominal composition and secondary nominal suffixes. Section three deals with the following fourteen sub-sections : morphology of the active voice, passive voice, perfect tense, benedictive, periphrastic future, simple future, conditional, aorist, various tenses of the passive, intensive medium, intensive active, secondary verbal derivative, irregular present stems and irregular formation of various tense. The section four has no sub-sections. It deals with primary nominative derivatives.

Though the name of the author has not been mentioned either in the text or in the colophon; still from the subsequent commentary (CH V/3) it is known that Anubhūtisvarūpācārya composed this work in 13th century A.D.

The translator of the this work i.e. *Ṅag-dbaṅ-phun-tshogs-lhun-grub* completed this work with the help of Balabhadra and Gokulanātha Misra, two Indian Pandits.[20] It is also known from the colophon that these two Indian Pandit were master in five seiences (*gnas-lṅa*). It is further known from the same source that the translator composed the work during the life-time of *Ṅag-gi-dbaṅ-phyug-blo-bzaṅ-rgya-mtsho,* the fifth Dalai Lama, to whom he salutes in the colophon.[21]

Four translation works on skt. grammar are ascribed to our translator.[22] He was one of the main exponents of the last phase of flourishing of translating activities in Tibet. A total number of nine translations in the Peking *bstan-'gyur* are credited to him.

The present translation was completed by the translator at Potala in 1665 A.D.?

Balabhadra was the older brother of Gokulanātha Miśra and these two brothers were great scholars of Sanskrit grammar in 17th century A.D. These two brothers were Brahmin by caste and resided in Lhasa for several years in the middle of the 17th century A.D. It is known from the colophon of the work CH II/4 that these two Brahmin Paṇḍits were from pure Brahmin family of Kurukṣetra, in Western India. But Kurukṣetra is a religious place in the modern Hariyana State of Northern India. Again some other sources suggest that these two brothers were from Vārāṇasī.

The work was translated at Potala, the famous palace of the Dalai Lamas or the *dmar-po-ri* hill dominating Lhasa. This was also the site of earlier palaces, which however were superseded by the present structure. The building work of the palace was started about 1645 A.D. and continued till sometime after the death of the 5th Dalai Lama (1617 to 1682).

CH V/3

Title : *(brda-sprod-pa'i-bstan-bcos-chen-po-) dbyaṅs-can-byā-ka-ra-ṇa'i-'grel-pa-rab-tu-bya-ba-gsal-ldan (-zhes-bya-ba).*
"Commentary on the *Sarasvatī* grammar called *prakriyā-caturā*".
[Pek. 5912, Nā, 3904, De. 4298 and Co. SE 2].
Skt. : Sarasvatī-vyākaraṇa-vṛtti-prakriyā-caturā nāma.
Author : Anubhūti (svarūpācārya).
Translator/s : Balabhadra, Gokulanātha Miśra and *'dar-nag-dbaṅ-phun-tsogs-lhun-grub.*
Place : Potala
Date : 17th century A.D.

This is a commentary on the *Sarasvata* system of Sanskrit grammar. The subject matter and the construction of the whole text is like that of the previous text (CH V/2). Now it is not necessary to mention the contents of the text again. Though in the CH V/2, the name of the author has not been mentioned, still in the present text the author is described in the colophon as the great master in the five sciences Anubhūti (svarūpcārya) (i.e. in Tibetan : *rjes-su-'byor-pa-raṅ-bzhin-bzaṅ-po).*[23] Now it may not be out of context to mention that like the previous text (i.e. CH V/2) separate xylographical editions of the present translation existed, *e.g. those of the dga-ldan-phun-tshogs-glin*[24] and *zhol-par-khan*[25] printing houses.

Refer CH V/2 for the life-history of Balabhadra. Gokulanāth Miśra was an Indian scholar who had spent several years in Lhasa during middle of 17th century A.D. Balabhadra, the other translator of this text was his brother. These two brothers from India had translated the present text into Tibetan along with *'dar Nag-dban-phun-tshogs-lhun-grub.* It is known from the colophon of the text CH II/4 that both the brothers haild from Kurukṣetra of modern Hariyana. But we have no evidences to prove that there was a monastery at Kurukṣetra during middle 17th century A.D. However, from other sources it is known that they haild from Varanasi and had gone to Tibet during the age of the fifth Dalai Lāmā. It is quite possible that Varanasi was the birth place of these two scholars as the tradition of Sanskrit Learning was active there during middle 17th century A.D. and again it helps our suggestion that there is still a great monastery near Varanasi. However, these two brothers were expert in both Pāṇinian and Sārasvata systems of grammar.

Refer CH V/2 also for the history and achivements of *'dar Nag-dbaṅ-phun-tshogs-Ihun-grub.*

Notes and References

1. Cf; iti śrīnarendrācārya Sārasvate kṣemendrakṛtam ṭippaṇam samāptam/vide, Belvalkar, S.K; 1915, p. 79. This standpoint of kṣemendra is also supported by Amṛtabhārati, another commentator of the Sārasvata-prakriyā (Ibid).
2. Refer, Ibid, p. 77 (note 1).
3. Refer, Coward, H.G. and Raja, K, (Ed.) Encyclopedia of Indian philosophies, vol. V, Delhi, 1990, p. 20.
4. Cf; *sārasvatīmṛjum kurve prakriyām nātivistāram//* The introductory verse 1 of the Sārasvataprakriyā.
5. Refer, Chandra, L; (Ed); Koṅgtrul's Encyclopaedia of Indo-Tibetan Culture, with an Introduction by E. Gene Smith, 1970, Vol. 1 : 35. 2, 556.1 and 556.2.
6. Ibid, 35.2.
7. Ibid, 556.5.
8. Scharfe, H; A History of Indian Literature (Grammatical Literature), vol. V, Fasc. 2, Wiesbaden, 1977, p. 189.
9. Cf; *pu-ñdza-rā-dza,* Chandra, L; 1970, vol. 1 : 556.5.
10. Refer, Belvalkar, S.K; 1915, p. 81.
11. Refer, Abhyankar, K.V; 1977, p. 252.
12. Ibid, p. 252.
13. Refer the colophon of CH V/2.
14. Refer, Chandra, L; 1970, vol. 1 : 556.4, 556.5.
15. Cf; *dbyaṅs-can-ma-brda-sprod-pa'i-mtshams-sbyor-'grel-pa-daṅ-bcas-pa-'di-paṇḍita-kṛṣṇabhaṭṭa-daṅ-tā-ra-nā-thas-bsgyur-ba'o//* [Pek. 312r4].
16. Schiefner, A; (Ed) Tāranāthae de doctrine buddhical in India propagatione narratio, Petropolis, 1868.

17. Cf; *bod-yul-du-jo-naṅ-rje-bstun-sgrol-ba'i-mgon-pos-paṇḍita-kṛṣ-ṇa-daṅ-ba-la-bha-dra-la-brten-nas-gzhuṅ-'grel-thog-mar-bsgyur/* Ed. Chandra, L; 1970, vol. 1 : 556-2-536-3.
18. Cf; 'grel-pa'aṅ-mdzad/Ibid, 556.3.
19. Refer Pek. 198 r1 to 206 v3.
20. */tshul-'di-srid-gsum-'gro-ba'i-gñen-gcig-pu*
/ṅag-gi-dbaṅ-phyug-blo-bzaṅ-rgya-mtsho-yi
/zhabs-zuṅ-gtsug-gi-rgyan-du [Pek. tu] *-rtag-mchod-pa*
/ke-dkar-rigs-skyes-rmoṅs-rtul-sñoms-las-pas /
/gnas-lṅa-mthar-soṅ-'phags-yul-paṇḍi-ta /
ma-hā-paṇḍita-ba-la-bha-dra-daṅ-paṇḍi-ta-go-ku-la
(Co. mā?)-nā-tha-miśra/mched-kyi-gsuṅ-rgyun-dri-med-legs-bsad-ltar /
/phun-tshogs-sde-bzhi'i-dṅos-kun-'du-ba'i-gnas /
rgyal-khab-chen-po-po-ta-lā-ru-bsgyur /
[Pek. 206 v3-5 ; Co. 9r4-5].
21. Refer the note above.
22. Cf; CH V/2-3 and CH II/3-4.
23. Pek. 341 v4, Co. 124 v5.
24. E.g. Van Manen collection, Leiden, reg. no. 2740/1 + 38.
25. E.g. Harrer collection, Museum fur Volkerkunde, Wien, reg. no. 132. 280.

6

MAÑJUŚRĪ ŚABDA-LAKṢAṆA, A NEW SYSTEM OF SANSKRIT GRAMMAR.

History of Mañjuśrīśabdalakṣaṇa :

The Mañjuśrī-śabda-lakṣaṇa or the Mañjuśrī-śabda-vyākaraṇa do not appears in the works of Bu-ston and Tāranātha. Koṅ-sprul only suggests that the basic text of this system is attributed to Mañjuśrīkīrti.[1] But in the colophon of the text (i.e. CH VI/1) it has been mentioned that the *sūtra*-text of the grammatical system of Mañjuśrī personally expounded by the monk Sādhukīrti, a master of great learning thanks to the grace of noble *Mañjuśrīkīrti*, has now been fully completed viz., *dpal-ldan-'jam-dpal-dbyaṅs-kyi-byin-gyis-brlabs-pa'i-mkhas-pa-chen-po // slob-dpon-dge-sloṅ-legs-par-grags-pa'i-zhal-sṅa-nas-bkod-pa-'jam-dpal-gyi-brda-sprod pa'i-mdo-yoṅs-su-rdzogs-so //* [Pek. 42 v1-2]. Koṅ-sprul, further, mentions that the work consists of eight sections (Tib. *skabs*) of four sub-sections (Skt. *pāda*, Tib. *rkaṅ-pa*) each. Thus, the total number of sub-sections are thirty-two, which are equal to the Aṣṭ. of Pāṇini.

Ko. also mentions a commentary which comments upon only the first two *pādas* of the fifth section of the basic text. This voluminous commentary, entitled *Aṣṭasāhasrikā-vṛtti-mañjuśrī-śabda-vyākaraṇa* (i.e. CH VI/2), is found in the canonical editions and indeed comments upon the *sūtra*-text up to the end of second sub-section of fifth section.[2]

In the canonical translation this commentary is attributed to *'rgyal-po'i-lha* (Rājadeva?),[3] king-scholar of the country of the *Boddhisattva*, noble sovereign of Kaliṅga, viz., *khes-pa-sā-dhu-*

kī (Co. gi)-rtti'i-'jam-dpal-gyi-brda (Co. sgra-brda) -sprod-pa-dpal-ldan-ka-linga'i-dbaṅ-phyug-byaṅ-chub-sems-dpa'i-yul-gyi-slob-dpon-rgyal-po'i (Co. rgyal-po'i) -lhas-rnam-par-bkod-pa-stoṅ-phrag-brgyad-pa-las-skabs-lṅa-pa'i-rkaṅ-pa-gñis-pa'i-'grel-pa-rdzogs-so //

[Pek. 197 v3-4 ; Co. 296 r1-2].

Ko. states that both, the basic text and the commentary have been translated by the translator from *zha-lu*, called *chos-skyoṅ-bzaṅ-po*, the famous grammarian and translator. This translator is also known by the Sanskrit version of his ordination name, viz., Dharmapālabhadra (1441-1527).[4] On the basis of the date of the translator, we may opine that the work was translated in between the last quarter of 15th century A.D. to 1st quarter of the 16th century A.D. A close study of the Ms. suggests that this translation of the text has some similarity with the Cāndra system of the Sanskrit grammar. This suggestion is also supported by the colophon. In the colophon it has been categorically mentioned that the translator had gone through the Cāndra sūtras before translating the present text. He not only had gone through the Cāndra-sūtras, but a comparison between the present text and the Cāndra-sūtras was done by the translator before beginning his translation work of this Ms.

CH VI/1 :

Title : *Jam-dpal-gyi-sgra'i-mtshan-ñid*
"The description of language of Mañjuśrī"
[Pek. 5909, Nā; 3901 and De. 4433].
Skt : *Mañjuśrī-śabda-lakṣaṇa*
Author : Sādhukīrti
Translator : Dharmapāla (bhadra)
Place :
Date : 15th/16th century A.D.

This system of Sanskrit grammar is not known in the history of Sanskrit grammar in India. Only two works of this system are exist in the Tibetan translation works. The present work contains the short prescriptive sūtras and the following text (i.e. CH VI/2) is an incomplete commentary on the sūtra-text.

The work is divided into eight sections and each section is divided again into four pādas. This work seems to be closely related with Cāndra system. The ordering of the sūtras in this text is like that of the Cāndravyākaraṇa sūtra of Candragomin (CH II/1). Like the Cāndravyākaraṇa, this text may be broadly divided into two parts. The first part deals with morphology and the later part deals with morphophonemics. The former part is incorporated with the following topics : I.1 to III.1 deal with primary suffixes;[5] III.2 deals with case semantics (*kārakas*);[6] III.3 deals with nominal declension7 and III.4 with the formation of feminine stems;[8] IV.1 to VI.4 deal with secondary derivations (*taddítas*)[9] Besides, like Cāndra grammar in the beginning the author mentions the word *śabdalakṣaṇa*, 'description Language' and in the Śiva sūtras, the catalog of phonemes that precedes the text, the fifth sūtra reads *ha-ya-va-ra-laṇ*, just like in the *Cāndra Śiva sūtras*.[10] Further, the translator mentions in the colophon that he had done the translation only after comparing this text with its commentary (CH VI/2) and the basic text of Cāndra grammar.[11] Thus, we may opine that this new system of grammar which was not popular, I but originated in India was closely related to Cāndra system.

The present text contains sūtras that give definitions of grammatical technical terms (samjña)11; but in the Cāndra grammar separate definitions of technical terms (*samjñās*) do not occur in the basic text.[12] Candragomin avoids the use of technical terms the meaning of which is not self evident and the technical terms that are used simply are not defined in a sūtra.

It is known from the colophon that the author was Sādhukīrti (Tib. *legs-par-grags-pa*), who was a monk and teacher of great learning, thanks to the grace of the noble *Mañjuśrīghoṣa*.[13] In the Indian tradition, no such name like Sādhukīrti is know as a grammarian and therefore, it is not possible to access his personal like in any way. Again, the association of Mañjuśrī with grammatical works, as we see in the title of the present treatise, is quite proper, as Mahābodhisattva Mañjuśrī (Manjughoṣa) is-especially in the Tibetan traditions particularly associated with speech and language as conveyors of wisdom. He is therefore, is called *Vagīśvara* and *Vādirāja* 'master of speech'.

Refer CH II/12 for the translator.

CH VI/2 :

Title :*jam-dpal-gyi-sgra-brda-sprod-pa'i-grel-pa-stoṅ-phrag-brgyad-pa.*

"Commentary on the Mañjuśrī grammar entitled aṣṭasāhasrikā"

[Pek. 5910, Nā. 3902, De. 4280 and Co. RE 12].

Skt. Aṣṭasāhasrikā-vṛtti-mañjuśrī-śabda-vyākaraṇa.

Author : rgyal-po'i lha (Rājadeva).

Translator/s : zha-lu chos-skyon-bzaṅ-po Dharmapālabhadra.

Place : *gdan-sa-rin-po-che-thel and gra-thaṅ.*

Date : 15th/16th century A.D.

This is a commentary on the Mañjuśrī vyākaraṇa of Sādhukīrti.[14] It is not complete and deals with the basic text upto the end of the second sub-section of the fifth section.[15] Thus, it covers slightly more than half of the text.

It is known from the concluding phrases of each sub-section that the author *rgyal-po'i-lha* was a noble sovereign of Kaliṅga.[16]

The ancient Kaliṅga country seems to have comprised modern Orissa to the south of the Vaitaraṇī and the sea-coast southwards as far as Vizagapatam. It also included the Amarakanṭaka range which is said to be in its western part. (B.C. Law's, 1984, p. 157).

Refer CH II/12 for the Author.

The translation of this work was started at the monastery called *gdan-sa-rin-chen-thel* which was situated in the dense forest of *kun-tu-bzaṅ-po* and the translation was completed in the monastic academy of the noble monastery *grwa-than.*[17]

The location of the former monastery can be identified as the well-known monastery *gdan-sa-(m) thil*, head-monastery of the *phag-mo-gru-pa* branch of the *bka-brgyud-pa* sect, founded by *phag-mo-gru* in 1158,[18] situated in eastern dbus province, to the north of the *gtsaṅ-po* river, north of the *yar-luṅs* district.[19]

The *grwa-thaṅ* monastery was founded by the *gter-ston grwa-pa mṅon-ses* in 1081 A.D.[20] in a valley called grwa-nan in *dbu-ru,* south of the *gtsaṅ-po* river and west of the yar-k-luṅs district.[21] Besides, the two translations mentioned above, one more colophon in Peking *bstan-'gyur* refers to *grwa-thaṅ* as the place of the translation.[22]

Notes and References

1. Cf; *'jam-dpal-grags-pa*; Chandra, L (Ed.), 1970, vol. 1 556-6.
2. Refer CH VI/2 for detail.
3. The Tibetan word *rgyal-po'i-lha may* be reconstructed into Sanskrit as (*rgyal-po'i*) > *Rāja* + lha > *deva* = Rājadeva.
4. This view of Ko. also has been supported by the translator (See the colophon).
5. Refer Pek. 1v3 to 11r8.
6. Ibid; 11r8-v8.
7. Ibid; 11v8-13r7.
8. Ibid; 14r7-19v1.
9. While Pāṇini reads ha-ya-va-raṭ and laṇ as two separate sūtras, Cāndra reads ha-ya-va-ra-laṇ as one and a single sūtra. This is also found in the Mañjuśrī śabda-lakṣaṇa.
10. Cf; */di'i-'grel-daṅ-tsāndra-yi // gzhuṅ-la-gtugs-nas-legs-par-bsgyur* /[Pek. 42v3-4].
11. Cf; e.g. Liebich, B; Konkordanz Pāṇini-cāndra, 1928, Breslau, pp. 47-48.
12. Cf; *dpal-ldan-'jam-dpal-dbyaṅs-kyi-byin-gyis-brlabs-pa'i-mkhas-pa-chen-po / slob-dpon-dge-sloṅ-legs-pa-grags-pa'i-zhal-sṅa-nas-bkod-pa .... /*
    [Pek. 42v1-2]
13. Refer CH VI/1 above.
14. Cf; Pek. 42v4-197v3.
15. Refer. Pek, 197v 3-4 and Co-296r1-2.
16. Cf; *// 'di-ni-mkhyen-brtse-tshad-med-pa-mṅa'-ba'i-bdag-ñid / sprul-sku-rin-po-che-zhwa-dmer-cod-pan (Co. pa-na)-'dzin-pa-bzhi-pa / thoms-cad-mkhyen-pa-spyan-sṅa-rin-po-che'i-zha-sṅa-nas-sgyur (Co. bsgyur)-cig-ces-bka'-stsal-zhiṅ-mthun-rkyen-graṅ-ba-las / kha-lu-lo-tsā-ba-dge-sloṅ-dha-rma-pā-la-bha-dra-zhes-bgyi-bas-(Co. /) dpal-kun-tu-bzaṅ-po'i-nags-khrod-gdan-sa-rin-chen-thil (Co. rin-po-che-thel)-gyi-gzims-khaṅ-du-dbu-btsugs-nas / dpal-gra-thaṅ-gi-gtsug-lag-khaṅ-du-rdzogs-par-bsgyur-ba'o* /[Pek 197v4-b; Co. 296 r2-4].
17. Cf.; *deb-ther-sṅon-po*; Chandra, L; (Ed.); The Blue Annals, 1976, New Delhi, p. 488.
18. Refer; Cordier, P; Catalogue du Fonds tibetai de la Bibliothegue Nationale 3e partie : Index du *bstan-bgyur* (Tibetain 180-322), 1915, Paris, p. 516.

19. Cf. *deb-ther-snon-po : lcags-mo-bye-la-gra-thon-gi-rman-btin* /
20. Refer : Tucci, G; To Lhasa and Beyond, 1956, Roma, pp. 147-48.
21. Refer; Lalou, M (Ed): Repertoire du Tanjur d'apres le Catalogue de P. Cordier, avce une Preface de Paul Pelliot, 1933, Paris, p. 225

7

OTHER WORKS ON SANSKRIT GRAMMAR

Earlier, it has been mentioned that 47 Sanskrit grammatical treatises were translated into Tibetan by various scholars in different times. Out of these 47 works 41 treatises are affiliated to five grammatical systems i.e. Pāṇinian, Cāndra, Kātantra, Sārasvata and Mañjuśrī system. However, Bu-ston mentions about a grammatical text book which is unknown elsewhere, both in the Indian and Tibetan traditions. He says : "Thereafter the Paṇḍit Rājacrī has made a compendium of the Kalāpa and the Cāndra-vyākaraṇa; his work is known as the Rājacrī-vyākaraṇa".[1] This is not mentioned by Tāranātha and Koṅ-sphul. This Rājaśrī-vyākaraṇa has not referred by any scholar both from India and Europe. It is of course possible that Bu-ston intends the Mañjuśrī-vyākaraṇa which indeed follows both the Cāndra and the Kalāpa systems. If this Rājaśrī-vyākaraṇa is indeed the Mañjuśrī-vyākaraṇa, then this system of grammar was composed before 1322 A.D., the date of composition of Bu-ston's work.[2]

The rest six treatises are not affiliated to any system of Sanskrit grammar. These six works have been discussed in the present chapter for our practical purpose.

CH VII/1

Title : *smra-ba-kun-la-jug-pa'i-sgra'i-bstan-bcos.*
"A grammar for the correct usage of language"
"Pek. 5779, Nā. 3771, De. 4290 and Co. SE 4].
Skt. : *Sarvabhāṣā-pravartana-vyākaraṇa śāstra*

Author : Subhāṣakīrti
Translator/s : Not mentioned
Place : Not mentioned
Date : Before 14th. century A.D.

This is a brief metrical work on semantics and syntax of Indian Language, Presumably Sanskrit with twenty number of verses. It describes semantical and syntactic phenomena in such general terms, without explicitly referring to Sanskrit and without including morphological elements from the object language, that it is not self-evident that it is dealing with classical Sanskrit. It might be done for more than one Indian language. In the Indian traditions of linguistic philosophy we regularly meet with the statement of certain often semantical or syntactic-phenomena as Universals, i.e. valid for all languages, that are modelled on the semantical and syntax of Sanskrit as described by the science of grammar.[3] In this text the passages dealing with nominal compounds and case-relations are clearly based on the descriptions in the indigenous Indian systems of grammar.[4]

We get the name of the author of the work as Subhāṣakīrti, about whom no information seems to be available.5 The same author is also credited with another text (CH VII/2) which is a commentary on this metrical treatise. Thus, the author composed his own commentary on the present text.

CH VII/2

Title:*smra-ba-kun-la-jug-pa'i-sgra'i-bstan-bcos-kyi-'grel-pa.*
"Commentary on the grammar for correct usage of language".
[Pek. 5780, Nā. 3772, De. 4291 and Co. SE 5].
Skt. : Sarvabhāṣāvṛtti
Translator/s : Not mentioned
Place : Not mentioned
Date : Before 14th Century A.D.

This is an auto-commentary on the text mentioned just above. The work has four sections *(sbyor-ba)*. In the first two *adhyayas* the author deals with categorizations pertaining to speech, discourse and language in general *(rigs-kyi-'dom-pa-sel-*

ba).[6] Besides, the said two chapters bear variety of technical terms and category pertinent to semantics and syntax *(dus-kyi-dom-pa-sel-ba).*[7] The rest two chapters deal with a study on the intention and purpose of the correct usage of language *(ched-du-bya-ba)*[8] and a study on the *nāman (miṅ-du-btags-pa).*[9]

CH VII/3

Title : *ldog-pa-bsdus-pa-bstan-pa'i-tshig-le'ur-byas-pa*
"Verses containing a concise expose on negations"
[Pek. 5782, Nā. 3774, De. 4293 and Co. SE 7].
Skt : Piṇḍ-nivartana-nirdeśa-kārikā.
Author : Nabidharma/Nibidharma.
Translator/s : Not mentioned
Place : Not mentioned
Date : Before 14th century A.D.

According to the introductory verse,[10] the work is based on a number of Indian authorities and it is like a synopsis of semantics of negations. This work is in verse form. In this work grammarians like Pāṇini, Savyacandra or Candragomin, Ratnamati,[11] Pūṇacandra (Tib. *gaṅ-zla-ba*)[12] have been mentioned. It is also interesting to note that the mīmāmsā system has been referred to in this work.[13] The reference to the Mīmāmsakas as one of the sources indicates that the subject matter of the present text and its commentary (CH VII/4) lies within the domains of both linguistics and philosophy.

The Mīmāmsā system recognises two types of negation *prayyudāsa* (negation of a term which has a positive implication) and pratiṣedha (negation of a predicate without a positive implication). The grammarians also accept this division of negation as the Mīmāmsakas suggests. However, the grammarians call the later division as *prasajya-patiṣedha* (Tib. *med-par-dgag-pa*). It is precisely this dichotomy of negations that is dealt with rather elaborately in the present treatise and its commentary.

The whole treatise may be divided into four sections on the basis of the commentary; however, no such division is indicated in the text. The opening section (lines 1 to 40) gives a synoptic enumeration of the various types of the negations and the second section (lines 41 to 135) deals with the sub-division of negations in detail. The third one (lines 136 to 248) is incorporated with the scope or domain of various negations and the last section (lines 249 to 369) bears a study related to a further classification of various types of negation and their scope with suitable examples.

CH VII/4

Title : *ldog-pa-bsdus-pa-bstan-pa'i-mam-'grel.*
"Commentary on the concise expose on negations"
[Pek. 5783, Nā. 3775, De. 4294 and Co. SE 8].
Skt : Piṇḍa-nivartana-nirdeśa-vārttika.
Author : Nabidharma/Nibidharma.
Translator/s : Not mentioned
Place : Not mentioned
Date : Before 14th century A.D.

This is a commentary on the text mentioned just above. The commentary is written in prose and like the text it is not strictly confined with grammar, but paragrammatical as it deals with subject matter related to philosophy. The name of the author of this text has been mentioned Nibidharma[14] which seems to be unknown within the Indian grammartical traditions considering the subject matter of the text we may opine that the author was a philosopher; but nothing more be suggested due to lack of evidences.

CH VII/5

Title : *ner-bsgyur-gyi-mtshan-ñid-kyi-bśad-pa*
"Commentary on the characteristics of the verbal prepositions"
[Pek. 5786, and Nā. 3778].
Skt : Upasarga-lakṣaṇa-bhāṣya.
Author : Indradatta (dban-pos-sbyin-byin).
Translator/s : *nam-mkha-bzaṅ-po.*
Place : Not mentioned
Date : 14th century A.D.

This work does not belong to a particular school of Sanskrit grammar. It contains a study on twenty upasargas and, thus, it is similar to the previous work on upasargas discussed above under CH VII/2. Here we find the upasargas in a different order i.e. pra, upa, apa, ava, āṅ, parā, sam, ud, dur, nir, vi, ni, ati, pari, adhi, prati, api, abhi, su and anu. This order is not similar to that of other works on this subject. For example we find a different order in the work mentioned under CH III/2.

It is known from the colophon that the author of the work is Indradatta viz; *brda-sprod-pa-chen-po'i ghā-ṭā-pa'i-slob-dpon-dbaṅ-pos-byin-gyis-mdzad-pa'i-ñer-bsgyur-gyis-mtshan-nid-kyi-bśad-pa-rdzogs-so //.*[15] The word *dbaṅ-pos* means 'Indra' *byin* means 'giver' and thus we may reconstruct the word in Sanskrit as *'Indradatta'*: The original Sanskrit work of the present treatise is not available. The name Indradatta in the history of Sanskrit grammar is not so popular. A grammarian named Indradatta had composed two works named : Guḍhaphakkikāprakāśa and Samvādacintāmaṇi. The former one is a gloss on the difficult passages in the Siddhānta-kaumudī of Bhaṭṭoji Dikṣita and the later one is a small treatise on roots and their meanings. Besides, he is credited with a commentary on the Śabdakaustubha, named Kaustubhaguṇa.[16] This Indradatta was flourished during the later half of 18th century A.D.[17] It is known that the translator of the treatise under discussion was flourished in 14th century A.D. and therefore, the original Sanskrit work was prepared definitely before 14th century A.D. Now we may opine that the Indian grammarian Indradatta (18th century A.D.) is not identical with the author of this treatise and we have not evidences to prove that another Indradatta had composed the present work before 14th century A.D.

The translator *mam-mkha'-bzaṅ'po* was flourished during 14th century A.D. and he was a student of *byaṅ-chub-rtse-mo* and the teacher of *tsoṅ-kha-pa* and *thugs-rje-dpal,* a great translator of 15th century A.D. Three canonical treatises on Sanskrit grammar are translated by our translator including the present one.[18] The same scholar is also known to have contributed to six translations in Peking *Bstan-'gyur* : one in the tantra section and five in the sūtra section together with his teacher *byaṅ-chub-rtse-mo* and the Indian Scholar Sumanahśrī. He produced the famous translation of the Meghadutta of Kālidāsa.

CH VII/6

Title : *rkyen-gsum-bśad-pa*
"Commentary on three groups of suffixes"
[Pek. 5896, Nā. 3888 and De. 4432].
Skt : tri-pratyaya-bhāṣya.
Author : *ñi-māi-sniṅ-po.*
Translator/s : *roṅ-zom chos-kyi-bzaṅ-po* and *chos-kyi-śes-rab.*
Place :
Date : 11th century A.D.

This is a text dealing with the derivations produced with three groups of taddhita suffixes.[19] The three groups of suffixes, consisting of fifty-six,[20] twenty-seven[21] and eleven[22] suffixes respectively, are designated as spyi-la-jug-pa 'of general occurrence'; graṅs-med-pa '(forming) indeclinables' and dṅos-po '(expressing) verbal action'. The division of taddhita suffixes seems to be a new one as it is not common to either Pāṇiniya, Candra or Kalāpa systems. First of all the tripartite division of taddhita suffixes occurs in verse twelve of the matrical treatise known as the Vāraruca samgraha.[23] Some scholars consider that the present text is a commentary on the verse of the said work.

From the Sanskrit text of Vāraruca-samgraha it is known that the Sanskrit terms for the said three types of taddhita are called as : sāmānya-avyaya-and bhāvakhyā, which are similar for the Tibetan terms mentioned above.

Though in the colophon it has been mentioned that the work is affiliated to Kalāpa system,[24] still we do not agree with the view. In the introduction of the work the Cāndra system is referred to.[25] Judging by the terminology and the citation-forms of the suffixes it could pertain to the Pāṇiniya or Cāndra system.

The present treatise shows remarkable resemblance with the third chapter of the work entitled Sambandha-siddhaya-bhidhāna-prakriyā (CH. III/12). These two works comment upon the same basic verse, the same group of suffixes are dealt with the same tripartite division, but the commentary is different. It is to mark that CH III/12 is described in its colophon as "following the treatise on Sanskrit grammar written by the great master Candragomin". Thus the translator wants to opine that the said work belongs to Cāndra system. However, in the colophon of CH III/12 and CH VII/6, Ñi-māi-sñiṅ-po has been mentioned as the author of both the works.[27] This name of the author may be restored into Sanskrit as Sūryagarbha[28] or Sūryasāra.[29] But in the history of Sanskrit grammar, we have no such Indian name, with with we may identify this Tibetan grammarian.

In the well-known historiography deb-then-sṅon-po an elaborate account of the life and works of the translator is given. He is known to have met Atis'a who visited Tibet from 1042 to 1054. Now we may safely suggest the date of the translator as mid-eleventh century A.D. Our translator contributed eight translations to the tantra and two to the sūtra section of bstan-gyur. He was specialized in logic and grammar.

Notes and References

1. Refer; Obermiller, E; History of Buddhism (Chos-ḥbyung) by Bu-ston (Eng. trans.). Part IInd; Heidelbeng (Leipzig), 1932, p. 169.
2. Refer, Vostrikov, A.I.; Tibetan Historical Literature (translated from Russian by H.C. Gupta), Calcutta, 1970, p. 141.
3. This work may be compared with the Śabdaśakti-prakāśikā of Jagadiśa Bhattacharya.
4. It suggests the traditional terminology of the six types of Sanskrit compounds viz., 'bhu-maṅ-po (=bahuvrīhi), zlas-dbye (= dvandva), ba-gñis (=dvigu), de'i-skyes-bu (=tatpuruṣa), zad-par-m-'gyur (=avyayībhāva) and las-'dzin (=karmadhārya) [Pek. 229v5-6] also Cf; the Mahāvyutpatti 4726-4731, as well as traditional terminology for the case-relations (Pek. 229 v6-7), e.g. las (=karman), byed-pa (=karaṇa/kartṛ), 'brel-ba (=Sambandha) etc.
5. Cf;/sgra'i-bstan-bcos-smra-ba-kun-la-'jug-pa-zhes-bya-ba-sbyor-ba-bzhi-daṅ-ldan-pa-slob-dpon (Pek. sloon i.e. abbriviated for slob-dpon)-chen-po-su-bhā-ṣa-kī-rtis (Pek. rttis)-mdzad-pa-rdzogs-so//
   [Pek. 230 r2-3 and Co. 238 r5].
6. Cf; Pek. 230 v4-231 v7.
7. Cf; Pek. 231 v7-238 r1.
8. Cf; Ibid 238 r1-3.
9. Ibid 238 r3-5.

10. Cf; sgra-daṅ-bstan-bcos-mkhas-pa'i-mthar-gyur-pa/
/pā-ṇi-ni-daṅ-sa-bya-tsandra-daṅ-/
/ratna-ma-ti-gaṅ-zla-ba-daṅ-/
ni-mam-sa-ka-la-sogs-mkhan-po-yi.
dgag-pa'i-bye-brag-rgya-cher-bśad-pa-las /
dmam-pa'i-don-du-ñuṅ-zad-bstan-pan-'dod /
[Pek. 245 v7-8].
11. Ratnamati was a grammarian perhaps from ceylone in the 12th century or earlier, Cf; Csoma de Koros"s article : Enumeraton of Historical and grammatical works to be met with in Tibet, JASB; vol. VII, pt. 2, 1838, p. 147.
12. Pūrṇacandra, a grammaran of Cāndra system, has composed a commentary of Dhātupāṭha. Cf; Ibid.
13. Cf; Pek. ni-mam-sa-ka; Co. ni-man-sa-ka.
14. Cf; The colophon of text : ldog-pa-bsdus-pa-bstan-pa'i-rban-'grel-slob-dpon-ni-bi-dharmas (Co. na-bi-dharmās)-blo-dman-pa'i-don-ched-du-gsal-tshig-tu-byas-pa-rdzog-so // [Pek. 273v8, Co. 279r7].
15. Pek. 319r7.
16. Refer, Abhyankar, K.V; 1986; p. 72.
17. Refer the Index to the Encyclopedia of Indian Philoophies Vol. V.
18. Besides the present work our translator had translated the texts like CH III/15 and CH IV/12.
19. We may assume this treatise to be a commentary on one verse (scil. verse 12 on tadditas) from the metrical synopsis of Sanskrit grammar on which CH II/1 and CH III/12 are partial commentaries.
20. Pek. 470v2-476r1.
21. Ibid; 476r1-477v8.
22. Ibid; 477v8-479r4.
23. Cf; sāmānyāvyayabhāvākhyas trividhas taddhito mataḥ/The Vāraruca /Samgraha, Ed, T. Ganapati Shatri, Trivandrum, 1913, verse 12ab, p. 30.
24. //'brel-ba-grub-pa'i-rkyen-zhes-bya-ba'i-le'u/slob-dpon-mkhas-pa-chen-po-khyad-par-du-rjod-byed-rnam-par-dag-pa'i-sgra-la-mkhas-pa-ñi-ma'i-sñiṅ-pos-byā-ka-ra-na-las-phyuṅ-ste-mdzad-pa/ka-la-pa'i-rtse-ba'i-don-gsal-bar-byed-pa/sam-sgra-ta'i-skad-kyi-de-kho-na-ñid-'chugs-med-par-ston-pa'i-rab-tu-byed-pa/sgra-bsgyur-gyi-lo-tsā-ba-roṅ-zom-chos-kyi-bzaṅ-po-daṅ/dge-sloṅ-chos-kyis-śes-rab-gñis-kyi-bod-skad-daṅ-sbyar-nas-don-ji-lta-bar-bsgyur-ba-ni/da-duṅ-bstan-pa-dus-yun-riṅ-du-gnas-par-gyur-na-gzhan-la-phan-par-sems-pas-lhag-pa'i-

bsam-pas-bka'i-b cad-la-ma-'das-par-bsgyur-ba-o/de-ñid-bod-skad-ñid-la-'jug-pa'i-tshul-tshig-gi-lhad-med-pa-gcig-kyaṅ-brjed-byaṅ-du-guṅ-na-bdag-gis-raṅ-ñid-khis-bkod-nas-yod-do/ rkyen-gsum-bśad-pa'i-rab-tu-byed-pa/zhes-bya-ba-rdzogs-so / [Pek. 479r5-8].

25. Cf; Liebich, B; Das Cāndra-vyākaraṇa. Phil-hist. Klasse 3, 1895, p. 307.
26. legs-par-sbyar-ba'i-skad-kyi-brda-sprod-pa'i-bstan-bcos-slob-dpon-chen-po-tsandra-go-mis-mdzad-pa'i-rjes-su-'braṅs-te/ [Co. 114 r4].
27. Please refer note 24 above.
28. Refer; Liebich, B; 1895, p. 308.
29. Ibid, p. 308.

BIBLIOGRAPHY

Abhyankar, K.V. (& Shukla, J.M. 1977). A Dictionary of Sanskrit Grammar, Baroda.

Aoki, B. (1955), Study on early Tibetan chronicls, Nippon Gakujutsu shinkokai, Tokyo.

Bechwith, C.I. (1987), The Tibetan Empire in Central Asia: A History of the Struggle for Great Power among Tibetans, Turks, Arabs and Chinese during the Early Middle Ages, Princeton.

Bell, charles (1968). Tibet past and present, London.

Belvalkar, S.K. (1915). An account of the different existing systems of Sanskrit grammar, being the Vishwanath Narayan Mandlik gold medal prize essay for 1909, Poona.

Bhattacharya, B.P. (1962). A Study in Language and Meaning, Calcutta.

Bira, S. & Sukhbatar, O. (1979). 'On the Tibetan and Mongolian Translations of Sanskrit Grammaitcal Works', in: W. Morgenroth (ed.) Sanskrit and World Culture. Proceedings of the Fourth World Sanskrit Conference of the International Association of Sanskrit Studies, Weimar May 23-30, Berlin, 153-161.

Bohtlingk, O. (1987) 'Über die Grammatik Kātantra', ZDMG 41, 657-666.

Bronkhorst, J. (1981). 'Meaning Entries in Pāṇini's Dhātupātha', Journal of Indian Philosophy 9, 335-357.

Bronkhorst, J. (1983). 'On the History of Pāṇinan Grammar in the early Centuries following Patañjali, Journal of Indian Philosophy 11, 357-412.

Chand, A. (1982). Tibet: Past and Present (1660-1981), Streling Publishers Pvt. Ltd; New Delhi.

Cardona, G. (1976). Pāṇini. A survey of research, The first Indian edition (1980), Delhi.

Cardona, G. (1978). 'Still again on the History of the Mahabhasya', Annals of the Bhandarkar Oriental Research Institute 58-59, 79-99.

Cardona, G. (1988). Pāṇini. His Work and its Traditions, Volume One: Background and Introduction, Delhi.

Chakravarti, S.C. (ed.) (1918). The Bhāṣā-vṛtti, a commentary on Pāṇini's grammatical aphorisms excepting those which exclusively pertain to the Veda by Purushottamadeva; edited with annotations, Rajshahi. (=Savitarāya-smṛti-rakṣaṇa-grantha-mālā 1)

Chakravarti, S.C. (ed.) (1919). The Dhātu-pradīpa by Maitreya-rakṣita, edited with annotations, Rajshahi (= Savitarāya-smṛti-rakṣaṇa-grantha-mālā 2)

Chandra, L. (1959). 'Tibetan Works printed by the Shoparkhang of the Potala', in: Jñānamuktāvalī Commemoration Volume, New Delhi, 120-132.

Chandra, L. (1961). 'Les imprimeries tibetaines de Drepung, Derge et Pepung', Journal Asiatiqu 249, 503-517.

Chandra, L. (1963). Materials for a History of Tibetan Literature, New Delhi. (=Śata-Piṭaka Series 28-30).

Chandra, L. (ed.) (1965-71). The Collected Works of Bu ston, Parts 1-28, New Delhi (=Śata-Piṭaka Series 41-68).

Chandra, L. (ed.) (1968). The Autobiography and Diaries of Si-tu paṇ-chen. With an introduction by E. Gene Smith, New Delhi. (=Śata-piṭaka Series 77).

Chandra, L. (1970). Kongtrul's Encyclopadia of Indo-Tibetan Culture. With an introduction by Ee. Gene Smith, Parts 1-3 New Delhi. (= Śata-Piṭaka Series 80-82).

Chandra, L. (1973). The Collected Works of Longdol Lama. Parts 1,2 New Delhi. (= Śata-Piṭaka Series 100)

Chandra, L. (1976). The Blue Annals, completed in A.D. 1478 by Hgos-lotsawa Gzhon-nu-dpal (1392-1481), New Delhi. (= Śata-Piṭaka Series 212)

Chandra, L. (1983). Catalogue of the Peking Tanjur, 4 vols., New Delhi. (= Śata-Piṭaka Series 325-328)

Chatterjee, D.C. (ed.) (1944). Sanskrit-Tibetan-English Vocabulary, being an edition and translation of the Mahāvyutpatti by A. Cosma de Koros, Part III, Calcutta. (=Royal Asiatic Society of Bengal)

Chatterji, K.C. (ed.) (1953-1961). Cāndravyākarana of Candragomin, part 1 (Chapters 1-3), Poona 1953, part 2 (Chapter 4-6), Poona 1961.

Cordler, P. (1915). Catalogue du Fonds Tibetain de la Bibliotheque Nationale 3e Partie: Index du Bstanhgyur (Tibetan 180-332), Paris.

Coward, H.G.; and Raja, K; The philosophy of Grammarians 1990, Delhi.

Csoma de Koros, A. (1838). 'Enumeration of Historical and Grammatical Works to be met with in Tibet', JASB 7, 2, 147ff. (=repr. JPASB 7 (1911), Extra No., 81-87)

Dagyab, L.S. (1966). Tibetan Dictionary. Bod-brda'i-tshig-mdzod, Dharamsala.

Das, S.C. (1902). A Tibetan-English Dictionary with Sanskrit Synonyms, Calcutta. (repr. Delhi 1972)

Das, S.C. (1915). An Introduction to the Grammar of the Tibetan Language with the text of Situ Sumtag, Dag-je Sal-wai Melong and Situi Shal lung, Darjeeling.

Dash, N.K; (1991). Puruṣottamadeva As Grammarian, Delhi.

Dash, N.K; (1992) An Encyclopaedic Dictionary of Indian Culture, Delhi.

Dash, N.K. (1991), Education in Ancient India as known from Pāṇini, K.V. Saudara Rajan Felicitation Volume, Delhi, vol. 1, 453-459.

Dash, P.C. (1986) A Comparative Study of the Paninian and Candra Systems of Grammar (Kṛdanta Portion), Delhi.

Demo, N.G. (ed.) (1972-1974). The collected works of 'Jam-dbyaṅs-bzhad-pa'i-rdo-rje, reproduced form prints from the Bkra-śis-khyil blocks, 15 vols., New Delhi. (=Gedan Sungrab Minyam Gyunphel Series 40-54).

Deshpande, M. (1979). 'Candragomin's Syntactic Rules. Some Misconceptions', Indian Linguistics 40, 133-145.

Dwivedi, J.N (1987), Samskṛt ke Bauddha Vaiyākaraṇa (in Hindi) Saranatha.

Dvarikadas Shastri (ed.) (1971). Bhāṣāvṛtti (a commentary on Pāṇini's grammar) by Purusottamadeva, Varanasi. (=Prachya Bharti Series 9)

Edgerton, F. (1953). Buddhist hybrid Sanskrit grammar and dictionary. 2: Dictionary, New Haven.

Eggeling, J. (ed.) (1874-1878). The Kātantra with the commentary of Durgasimha, fasc. I-VI, Calcutta. (=Bibliotheca Indica New Series nr. 297, 298, 308, 309, 396, 397).

Eimer, H. (1983). Some results of recent Kanjur research, Sankt Augustin. (=Archiv Fur Zentraliasiatische Geschichtsforschung 1)

Eimer, H. (ed.) (1988). Indology and Indo-Tibetology. Thirty years of Indian and Indo-Tibetan Studies in Bonn. / Indologie und Indo-Tibetologie. Dressing Jahre indische und indotibetische Studien in Bonn., Bonn. (=Indica et Tibetica 13)

Faddegon, B. (1929). 'The Mnemotechnics of Pāṇini's Grammar I: The Śiva-Sūtra', Acta Orientalia 7, 48-65.

Francke, A. H. (1926). Antiquities of Indian Tibet, 2 vols; (rpr. 1972, New Delhi).

Ghosh, B. (1970). 'Study of Sanskrit Grammar in Tibet', Bulletin of Tibetology 7, 2, 21-41.

Goldstein, M. (1979). Tibetan English Dictionary of Modern Tibetan, Kathmandu. (=Bibliotheca Himalayica II.7)

Gulik, R.H. van (1955). Siddham. An Essay on the History of Sanskrit Studies in China and Japan, Nagpur. (repr. New Delhi 1980)

Hahn, M. (1972). 'Some remarks concerning an edition of the Tibetan translation of the drama Lokananda by Candragomin", Indo-Iranian Journal XIII, 104-112.

Hahn, M. (1974). Candragomin's Lokanandanataka. Nach dem tibetischen Tanjur herausgegeben und ubersetzt. Ein Beitrag zur klassischen indischen Schauspieldichtung, Wiesbaden. (=Asiatische Forschungen 39)

Hasrato, B.J. (1970). History of Nepal Hoshiarpur (Punjab).

Heyes, R.P. (1983). 'Jinendrabuddhi', JAOS 103, 4, 709-717.

Inaba, S. (1955). 'The influence of Indian grammar on the development of Classical Tibetan grammar', Indogaku Bukkyo-gaku Kenkyu III, 2 [=6], 432-440.

Iyer, K.A. Subramania; (1969). Bhartṛhari: a study of the Vākyapadiya in the light of ancient commentaries, Poona. (=Deccan College Building Centenary and Sliver Jubilee Series 68)

Jackson, D.P. (1983A). 'Notes on Two Early Printed Editions of Sa-skya-pa Works', Tibet Journal VIII, 2, 3-24.

Jackson, D.P. (1983B), 'Commentaries on the Writings of Saskya Pandita: A Bibliographical Sketch', Tibet Journal VIII. 3, 3-23.

Jackson, D.P. (1987). The Entrance Gate for the Wise (Section III). Sa-skya Pandita on Indian and Tibetan Traditions for Pramāṇa and Philosophical Debate, 2 vols., (=Winener Studien zur Tibetologie und Buddhismuskunde 17)

Jackson, D.P. (1989). The 'Miscellaneous Series' of Tibetan Text in the Bihar Research Society, Patna. A Handlist, Stuttgart. (= Tibetan and Indo-Tibetan Studies 2).

Jha, A. & Choudhary, G.R. (1965). The Catalogue of the Tibetan Texts in the Bihar Research Society, Patna. Volume I (Miscellaneous series), Patna.

Keith, A.B. (1928). A History of Sanskrit Literature, Oxford.

Khetsun Sangpo [Mkhas-btsun-bzaṅ-po] (1973-1980). Biographical Dictionary of Tibet and Tibetan Buddhism, 11 vols. Dharamsala.

Keilhorn, L.F. (ed.) (1880-1885). The Vyākaraṇa-mahābhāṣya of Patañjali, 3 vols.,Bombay.

Kiparsky, P. (1982). Some theoretical problems in Pāṇini's grammar, Poona (=Post-graduate and Research Department Series 16).

Kyi, A.S. and Arts, M. (1980) ed., Tibetan Studies in honour of H. Richardson, Vikas Publishing House, Gaziabad, U.P.

Lalou, M. (1933). Repertoire du Tanjur d'apres le catalogue de P. Cordire, avec une preface de Paul Pelliot, Paris.

Lalou, M. (1939). Inventaire des Manuscripts tibetains de Touenhouang conserves a la Bibilotheque Nationale t. 1: (Fonds Pelliot tibetain) nos. 1-849, Paris.

Lalou, M. (1953). 'Les textes bouddhiques au temps du roi Khrisron-lde-bcan. Contribution a la bibliographie du Kanjur et du Tanjur'., Journal Asiatique 241, 313-353.

Lama Chimpa and Nagwag Nima; (1966). Life of Dipankara Śrījñāna, Calcutta.

Lama Chimpa and Chattopadhyāya, A; (1970). Tāranātha's History of Buddhism in India, Simla.

Liebich, B. (1895). 'Das Cāndra-Vyākaraṇa', Nachrichten der Konigl. Gesellschaft d. Wissenschaften z. Gottingen, Phil.-hist. Klasse 3, 272-321.

Liebich, B. (ed.) (1902). Cāndra-Vyākaraṇa. Die Grammatik des Candragomin Sūtra, Uṇādi, Dhātupātha, Lipzig.

Liebich, B. (ed.) (1918). Cāndra-vṛtti Der Original—Kommentar Candragomins zu seinem grammatischen Sūtra, Leipzig.

Liebich, B. (1919A). Zur Einfuhrung in die indische einheimische Sprachwissenschaft I: Das Kātantra, Heidelberg.

Liebich, B. (1919B). Zur Einfuhrung in die indische einheimische Sprachwissenschaft II: Historische Einfuhrung und Dhatupatha, Heidelberg.

Liebich, B.(1920A). Zur Einfuhrung in the die indische einheimische Sprachwissenchaft III: Der Dhatupatha, Heidelberg.

Liebich, B.(1920B). Zur Einfuhrung in the die indische einheimische Sprachwissenchaft IV: Analyse der Candra-Vrtti, Heidelberg.

Liebich, B. (1921). Materialien zum Dhatupatha, Heidlberg.

Liebich, B. (1928). Konkordanz Panini-Candra, Breslau.

Liebich, B. (ed.) (1930). Ksiratarangini, Ksirasvamin's Kommentar zu Panini's Dhatupatha, Breslau.

Luders, H. (1930 repr. 1940). 'Kātantra und Kaumāralāṭa', Sitzungsberichte Preuss. Akademie d. Wissenschaften (Phil.-hist. Klasse) Berlin, 1930, 482-538 (& Tafel 8, 9). (repr. in: Philogica Indica. Ausgwahlte Klein Schriften von H. Luders, Gottingen 1940, 659-721.)

Luders, H. (1940 repr.) 1973). 'Nachtrage zum Kaumāralāṭa', ZDMG 94 (1940), 25-33. (repr. in: Von Hinuber (ed.), H. Luders, Kleine Schriften, Wiesbaden, 1973, 27-35).

Manen, J. van (1922). 'A Contribution to the Bibliography of Tibet', Journal & Proceedings Asiatic Society of Bengal (N.S.) 18, 8, 445-525.

Mibu, T. (1967). A comparative list of the Tibetan Tripitaka of Narthang edition (Bstan-hgyur division) with the Sde-dge edition, Tokyo.

Miller, R.A.(1962). 'The Si-tu Mahapandita on Tibetan Phonology', in: To Dr. Hachiro Yuasa: A Collection of Papers commemorating his Seventieth Anniversary, Tokyo, 921-933. (repr. with addenda et corrigenda Miller 1976: 19-31).

Miller, R.A. (1963). 'Thom-mi Sambhoṭa and his Grammatical Tratises', Journal of the American Oriental Society 83, 485-502. (repr. with addenda et corrigenda Miller 1976: 1-18).

Miller, R.A. (1964). 'A Twelfth Century Tibetan Grammatical Fragment', T'oung Pao 51, 72-84. (repr. with addenda et corrigenda Miller 1976: 57-70).

Miller, R.A. (1965). 'Some Minor Tibetan Grammatical Fragments', ZDMG 115, 327-340. (repr. Miller 1976: 71-84).

Miller, R.A. (1966). 'Buddhist Hybrid Sanskrit āli, kāli as Grammatical Terms in Tibet', Harvard Journal of Asiatic Studies 26, 125-147. (repr. with addenda et corrigenda Miller 1976: 33-56)

Miller, R.A. (1976). Studies in the Grammatical Tradition in Tibet, Amsterdam.

Miller, R.A. (1980), 'Phone, phoneme and graph in the old Tibetan grammarians', Acta Orientalia Hungarica 34, 153-162.

Miller, R.A. (1983). 'Thon mi Sambhoṭa and his grammatical treatises reconsidered'. in: E. Steinkellner & H. Tauscher (eds.), Contributions on Tibetan Language, History and Culture. Proceedings of the Csoma de Koros Symposium held at Velm-Vienna, Austria, 1981, vol. 1, Wien, (= Wiener Studisn zur Tibtaologie und Buddhismuskunde 10), 183-205.

Miller, R.A. (1988). 'The First Two Tibetan Grammatical Treatiss as Known to the Sa skya Pandita' in: Uebach & Panglung (eds.) (1988: 263-278).

Miller, R.A. (1990). 'Case-grammar in the first two Tibetan grammatical treatises', in: L. Epstein & R.F. Sherburne (eds.), Reflections on Tibetan Culture, Essays in memory of Turrell V. Wylie, New York, (= Studies in Asian thought and religion 12), 187-204.

Mironoff, N.D. (ed.) (1911). Mahavyutpatti, St. Petersburg. (=Bibliotheca Buddhica 13).

Mishra, H. (1976). Cāndra-Vyākananạsya Samikṣātmaka Adhyayanam (Sanskrit), Delhi.

Monier-Williams, M. (1899). A Sanskrit-English Dictionary. Etymologically arranged with special reference to cognate Indo-European language, Oxford.

Mukhopadhyaya, S.K. (1944). 'Tibetan Translation of Prakriya-Kaumudi and the mention of Siddhanta Kaumudi therein', Indian Historical Quarterly 20, 63-69.

Nebesky-Wojkowitz, R. de (1958). 'Tibetan Blockprints and Manuscripts of the Museum of Ethnology in Vienna', Archiv fur Volkerkunde 13, 174-209.

Norbu, T.F. and Turnbull, C.M. (1969). Tibet, Chatto and windus, London.

Oberlies, T. (1989). Studies zum Candravyakarana. Eine kritische Bearbeitung von Candra IV.4.52-148 und v.2, Stuttgart. (=Alt-und Neu-Indische Studien 38).

Obermiller, E. (1931-32). History of Buddhism (Chos hbyung) by Bu-ston, 2 parts, Heidelberg.

Oppert, G. (ed.) (1894). The grammar of Sakatayana with the Prakriyasamgraha commentary of Abhayacandrasuri, published for the first time, Madras.

Palsule, G.B. (1955). A Concordance of Sanskrit Dhātupāthas, Poona.

Palsule, G.B. (1961). The Sanskrit Dhātupāthas—A Critical Study, Poona. (= Deccan College Dissertation Series 23).

Pansikar, W.L.S. (ed.) (1913). Siddhānta Kauumudī or Bhaṭṭoji Dikshita's vṛtti on Pāṇini's vyākaraṇa sūtras; containing Pāṇini's śhikshā, sūtrapāṭha, dhātupāṭha and liṅgānuśāsana with alphabetical list of sūtras and of all roots with pages, Bombay, (repr. New Delhi 1985).

Pradhan, P. (ed.) (1975) Abhidharmakosabhāṣyam of Vasubandhu, revised second edition with introduction indices etc., Patna.

Raghavan, V and others (1966-1978). New Catalogues Catologorum (10 vols.), Madras.

Rangacharya, M. & Varadarajingar, M.B. (eds.) (1916-1927). The Rupāvatāra of Dharmakīrti with additions and emendations for the use of college students, 2 vols., 1: Madras, 2: Bangalore.

Renou, L. (1940). La Durghaṭavṛtti de Śaranadeva, traite grammatical en sanskrit du xiie siecle, edite et traduit. Volume 1, fascicule I: Introduction, Paris. (Collection Emile Senart 6).

Renou, L. (1941-1956). La Durghaṭavṛtti de Śaranadeva, traite grammatical en sanskrit du xiie siecle, edite et traduit, 2 vols. in 5 fasc., (Collection Emile Senar).

Renou, L. (1942). Terminologie grammaticale du Sanskrit, 3 vols., Paris. (= Bibliotheque de 1'Ecole des Hautes Etudes, Sciences Historiqus et Phiologiques 280-281).

Renou, L. (1956). 'Etudes Panineennes III Les Unadisutra', Journal Asiatique 244, 155-165.

Renou, L. (1957). 'Grammaire et Vedanta', JA 245, 121-133. (=repr. in: Staal, 1972: 470-478).

Renou, L. & Filliozat, J. (1953). L'Inde Classique. manuel des tudes Indiennees, tome II, Paris-Hanoi. (=Bibliotheque de l'Ecole Francaise d'Extreme-Orient 3).

Richardson, H.E. (1962). Tibet and its History. Oxford University Press, London.

Roerich, G.N. (1949-1953). The Blue Annals (deb-ther-snon-po), 2 vols, Calcutta. (repr. in 1 vol., Delhi 1976).

Rona-Tas, A. (1968). 'A brief note on the chronology of the Tunhuang collections', Acta-Orientalia Hungarica XXI-3: 313-316.

Sakai Shiro (1955). 'Honyaku-myogidaishu no nangoshaku-Panjika-madhyavyutpatti ni tsuite [Some considerations about the Pañjikā-madhyavyutpatti]', Mikkyo Bunka (Quarterly Reports on the Esoteric Buddhism) 29-30, 66-57.

Sakaki, R. (ed.) (1916-1925). Mahāvyutpatti, part 1 & 2, Kyoto. (=Kyoto Imperial University Series 3).

Sankrtyayana, R. (1935). 'Sanskrit Palm-leaf Mss. in Tibet', JBORS XXI, 1, 21-43.

Sankrtyayana, R. (1937). 'Second Search of Sanskrit Plam-leaf Mss. in Tibet [with plates]', JBORS, XXIII, 1, 1-57.

Sankrtyayana, R. (1938). 'Search for Sanskrit Mss. in Tibet', JBORS XXIV, 4, 137-163.

Sankrtyayana, R. (1939). 'Chart of Letters in Sanskrit Mss. from Tibet', JBORS XXV, 1, 64-65.

Sarma, N.K. (ed.) (1935-1936). The Sāı asvata Vyākaraṇam of Anubhuti Svarupācārya, Benares, (repr. 1971).

Schiefner, A. (1848). 'Ueber die logischen und grammatischen Werke im Tandjur', Bulletin de la classe historico-philologique de l'Academie imp. ds sciences de St.-Petersbourg, 4, 284-302.

Schiefner, A. (ed.) (1868). Taranathae de doctrinae buddhicae in India propagatione narratio, Petropolis.

Schiefner, A, (1869). Tranatha's Geschichte des Buddhismus in Indian, St. Ptersburg.

Schubert, J. (1928-1929). 'Das Sum-cu-pa und Rtags-kyi-' ajug-pa des Lama Dbyans-can-grub-pa'i-rdo-rje. in Kommentar zu den gleichnamigen Schriften Thonmi Sam-bho-ta's ubersetzt und erklart. = Tibtische National grammatik, I. Teil (=Phil. Diss. Berlin)', Mitteilungen des Seminars fur orientalische Sprachen 31 (1928), 1-59 & 32 (1929), 1-54.

Shakabpa, T.W. (1967). Tibet: A Political History, New Haven & London.

Shastri, J.S. and Shastri, L. (1983-90). Catalogue of the Library of Tibetan works and Archives (manuscript Section); 2 vols., Dharmasala.

Shefts, . (1961). Grammatical method in Pāṇini: his treatment of Sanskrit present stems, New Haven. (=American Oriental Series Eassay 1)

Simonsson, N. (1957). Indo-tibetische Studien. Die methoden der tibetischen Ubersetzer, untersucht in Hinblick auf die Bedeutung inhrer Uberesetzungn fur die Sanskritphilologie, Uppsala.

Simonsson, N. (1982A). 'Reflections on the grammatical tradition in Tibet', in: Indological and Buddhist Studies. Volume in Honour of J.W. de Jong on his Sixtieth Birthday, Canberra, 531-544.

Simonsson, N. (1982B). 'On the concept of sentence in ancient Indian and Tibetan theory and on the function of case particles in Tibetan according to Tibetan grammarians', Fenno-Ugrica Suecana 5, 281-291.

Simonsson, N. (1986). 'A Note on the knowledge of Indian Grammar Among the Tibetan Translators of the Ninth Century', Orientalia Suecana 33-35 (1984-1986), 385-389.

Snellgrove, D.L. & Richardson, H.E. (1968). A Cultural History of Tibet, London.

Stall, F. (1962). 'Negation and the Law of Contradiction in Indian Thought', BSOAS 15, 52-71.

Stall, F. (D.) (1972). A Reader on the Sanskrit Grammarians, Cambridge Mass.-London.

Stein, R.A. (1962). Tibetan Civilization, Paris, (English translation 1972) London.

Suzuki, D.T. (1955-1961). The Tibetan Tripitaka, Peking edition, kept in the Library of the Otani University, Kyoto, 168 vols., Tokyo-Kyoto.

Tahikawa, M. (1983-88). Catalogue of the Library of Congress Collection of Tibetan Literature; in 2 pts.; (A Catalogue of the United States Library of Congress Collection of Tibetan Literature in Microfiche), Tokyo. Series Maior III and III b).

Takakusu, J. (trl.) (1896). A Record of the Buddhist Religion as Practised in India and Malay Archipelago, by I-Tsing, Oxford.

Tatz, M. (1976). 'On the Date of Chandragomin', in: H.C. Das, & C. Das & S.S.R. Palul (eds.), Buddhism and Jainism, part 2, Cuttack, 281-297.

Tatz, M. (1982). 'The Life of Candragomin in Tibetan Historical Tradition', Tibet Journal VII, 3, 3-22.

Taube, M. (1966) Tibetische Handschriften und Blockdrucke, 4 vols., Wiesbaden. (=Verzeichnis der Orientalischen Handschriften in Deutschland 9, 1-4)

Taube, M. (1978). 'Zu einingen Texten der tibetischen brda-gsar-rñin-Literature', in: E. Richter & M. Taube (eds.), Asienwissenschaftliche Beitrage—Johannes Schubrt in memoriam, Berlin (=Veroffentlichungen des Museums fur Volkerkunde zu Leipzing Heft 32), 169-201.

Tohoku (1934). Chibetto Daizokyo Somokuroku. A Compelete Catalogue of the Tibetan Buddhist Canons (Bkah-hgyur and Bstan-hgyur). Edited by H. Ui, M. Suzuuki, Y. Kanakura, T. Tada, Sendai.

Tohoku (1953). A Catalogue of the Tohoku Collection of Tibetan Works on Buddhism, Tohoku University.

Tripathi, S.N. (ed.) (1971). Śākaṭāyana-vyākaraṇam of Ācārya Śākatāyana (with the svopajna commentary, Amoghavrtti), Varanasi.

Trivedi, K.P. (ed.) (1915). Th Vaiyākaraṇabhuṣaṇa of Koṇḍabhaṭṭa with the Vaiyākaranabuṣaṇasāra and the commentary Kāśikā of Harirāma surnamed Kāla and with a critical notice of manuscripts, introduction, and critical and explanatory notes, Bombay. (=Bombay Sanskrit and Prakrit Series 70)

Trivedi, K.P. (ed.) (1925-1931). The Prakriyākaumudī of Rāmacandra (in two parts) with the commentary Prasāda of Viṭṭhala and with a critical notice of manuscripts and an exhaustive and critical introduction, Poona. (=Bombay Sanskrit and Prakrit Series 78, 82).

Tucci, G. (1933). Indo-Tibetica II. Rin c'en bzan po ela rinascita del Buddhismo in torno al mille, Roma.

Tucci, G. (1947). 'The Validity of Tibetan historical tradition', in: India Antiqua—J.Ph. Vogel Memorial Volume, Leiden, 309-322. [repr. in Opera Minora P. II, Roma 1971, 453-466].

Tucci, G. (1949). Tibetan Painted Scrolls, 3 vols., Roma.

Tucci, G. (1950). The Tombs of the Tibetan Kings, Roma.

Tucci, G. (1956). To Lhasa and Beyond , Roma.

Tucci, G. (1956-1971). Minor Buddhist Texts, Part I-III, Roma. (=Series Orientale Roma 9, 9-2, 43)

Tucci, G. (1957). 'The Fifth Dalai Lama as a Sanskrit Scholar' Sino-Indian Studies 5, 2350240. (repr. in: Opera Minora, P.II, Roma 1971, 589-594).

Vasu, S.C. (1891). The Aṣṭādhyāyi of Pāṇini, edited and translated into English, 2 vols, Allahabad.

Vedavrata (ed.) (1962-1963). Patañjali's Vyākaraṇa-mahābhāṣya with Kaiyaṭa's Pradīpa and Nagoji-bgaṭṭa's Uddyota, 5 vols., Gurukula Jhajjar (Rohatak).

Verhagen, P.C. (forthcoming A). 'Sanskrit grammatical literature in Tibet: a first survey', in: Panels of the VIIth World Sanskrit Conference—Kern Institute, Leiden: august 23-29, 1987 (gen. ed. J. Bronkhorst), vol. IX. Sanskrit Outside India (ed. J. G. de Casparis), Leiden 1991 (?), 47-62.

Verhagen, P.C. (forthcoming B). 'A ninth-century Tibetan summary of the Indo-Tibetan model of casesemantics', in: Proceedings of the Vth International Seminar on Tibetan Studies, Narita.

Verhagen, P.C. (forthcoming C). 'Tibetan expertise in Sanskrit grammar—a case-study: grammatical analysis of the term pratitya-samutpada', Journal of the Tibet Society, vol. 8(?).

Verhagen, P.C. (forthcoming D). 'The Mantra "Om manipadme hum" in an Early Tibetan Grammatical Treatise', Journal of the International Association for Buddhist Studies 13, 2.

Vostrikov, A.I. (1970). Tibetan Historical Literature, translated from the Russian by H.C. Gupta, Calcutta. (Indian studies past and present).

Wayman, A. (1988). 'The Tibetan Negativs med and ma-yin, and the Manjusri-nama-samgiti VI, 19 Commentaries', in: Uebach & Panglung (eds.) (1988: 551-558).

Wylie, T.V. (1962). The Geography of Tibet According to the 'Dzam-Gling-Rgyas-Bshad, Roma.

Yoshimizu, C. (ed.) (1989). Descriptive Catalogue of the Naritasan Institute Collection of Tibetan Works, Naritasan Shinshoji.

Yoshimura, S. (1950). The Denkar-ma, an oldest catalogue of the Tibetan Buddhist canons, Kyoto.

INDEX